CHAPTER I

INTRODUCTION—THE PRESENT UNREST IN EDUCATION

The problems as to the end or ends at which our educational agencies should aim in the training and instruction of the children of the nation, and of the right methods of attaining these ends once they have been definitely and clearly recognised, are at the present day receiving greater and greater attention not only from professed educationalists, but also from statesmen and the public generally. For, in spite of all that has been done during the past thirty years to increase the facilities for education and to improve the means of instruction, there is a deep-seated and widely spread feeling that, somehow or other, matters educationally are not well with us, as a nation, and that in this particular line of social development other countries have pushed forward, whilst we have been content to lag behind in the educational rear.

The faults in our present educational structure are many, and in some cases obvious to all. In the first place, it is said, and with much truth, that there is no systematic coherence between the different parts of our educational machinery, and no thorough-going correlation between the various aims which the separate parts of the system are intended to realise. As Mr. De Montmorency has recently pointed out, we have always had a national group of educational facilities, more or less efficient, but we have never had, nor do we yet possess, a national system of education so differentiated in its aims and so correlated as to its parts as to form "an organic part of the life of the nation."[1] An educational system should subserve and foster the life of the whole: it should be so organised as to maintain a sufficient and efficient supply of all the services which a nation requires at the hands of its adult members. For it is only in so far as the educational system of any country fulfils this end that it can be "organic," and can be entitled to the claim of being called a national system.

This lack of coherence between the different parts of our educational system and the want of any systematic plan or unity running through the whole is due to many causes. As a nation, we are little inclined to system-making, and as a consequence the problem of education as a whole and in its total relation to the life and well-being of the State has received but scant attention from politicians. Educational questions, in this country, are rarely treated on their own merits and apart from considerations of a party, political, or denominational character, and hence the problems which have received attention in the past and evoke discussion at the present are concerned with the nature of the constitution, and limits of the power of the bodies to whom should be entrusted the local control of the educational agencies of the country, rather than with the problems as to the aims which we should seek to realise through our educational organisation, and of the methods by which these aims may be best realised. Hence, as a nation, we have rarely considered for its own sake and as a whole the problem of the education of the children. And until we have done so—until we have made clear to ourselves the kind of future citizen which as a State we desire to rear up—our educational agencies must manifest a like indefiniteness, a like inconsistency, and a like want of connection as do our educational aims and ideals.

Again, closely connected with this first-named defect in our educational organisation, and in fact following from it as a logical consequence, is our fatal method of developing this or that part of our educational system and of leaving the other parts to develop, if at all, without any central guidance or control, until at length we realise that the neglected parts also require attention, and must somehow or other be refitted into the whole. *E.g.*, since 1870 there has been a great advance in the extent and intent of elementary education in both England and Scotland, but this progress has been of a one-sided nature, and there has been no corresponding advance either in the perfecting of the educational system as a whole, or in the co-ordination of the various grades of education. In Scotland, since the passing into law of the Education Bill of 1872, the means of elementary education have been widely extended and the methods of teaching have been greatly improved, but there has been no corresponding advance in the provision of the means of higher education, and as a consequence, at the present day, we find many districts without adequate provision for carrying on the education of the youth of the country beyond the Primary School stage. Secondary education has been provided in some centres by means of endowments; in others through the extension of the term "elementary" so as to include education of a more extended nature than was originally intended to be covered by that term. In England until 1902, very much the same conditions prevailed, but since then, mainly in order to remedy the state of things created by the judgment in the Cockerton Case, the control of primary, secondary, and technical education has been placed in the hands of the County and Borough Councils, who are empowered "to consider the educational needs of their area, and to take such steps as seem to them desirable, after consultation with the Board of Education, to supply or aid the supply of education other than elementary, and to promote the general co-ordination of all forms of education." Tinder the powers so granted much has been done throughout England during the past few years to extend and make efficient the means of higher education; to erect schools which shall provide training for the future services required by the community and the State of the more highly gifted of its members, and to co-ordinate the work of the various agencies entrusted with the care and education of the children of the nation.

Through the failure of the Education Bills of 1904 and 1905 to pass into law, Scotland still awaits the creation of local authorities charged with the control and direction of all grades of education, and in this respect her educational organisation is much more loosely compacted than the system which now exists in England.

Further, in Scotland, on account of the absence of one controlling authority, we often find in those districts in which the provision for higher education is ample, imperfect co-ordination between the aims and work, on the one hand, of the Primary School, and on the other, of schools providing higher education. From this cause also it follows that, unlike our German neighbours, we have made little progress in determining the different functions which each particular type of Higher School shall perform in the social organism, and have not assigned the particular services which the State requires of each particular type of Higher School. It is surely manifest that the service which the modern industrial State looks for from its members is not the same in kind and is much more complex in its nature than that which was required during the mediæval period, and that if this service is to be efficiently supplied, then there is need for Higher Schools varied in type and having various aims.

This want of unity between the various parts of our educational system manifests itself again in the indefiniteness of aim of many of our Higher Schools, and in the lack of co-ordination between the Higher School on the one hand, and institutions providing university and advanced instruction on the other. Up till quite recently, the sole aim of our Secondary Schools was to provide students for the Universities and to supply the needs of the learned professions. But with the economic development of the country, and as a consequence of the keen international competition between nation and nation in the economic sphere, there has arisen a demand for a higher education different in kind from that provided by the older Universities, and a need for a type of Secondary School different in aim and curriculum from that which looks mainly to the provision of students intending to enter upon some one or other of the so-called well recognised learned professions. It is here, when compared and contrasted with the educational systems of some of our Continental neighbours, that we find the weakest point in our own system, and at the present time our most urgent need is for the extension and better equipment of the central institutions of the country which provide higher technical and commercial instruction.

This unsatisfactory condition of things is due in large measure, as we have already pointed out, to our innate dislike as a nation of all system-making, and to the distrust felt by many minds of any and every form of State control of education. Hence, partly from these causes, partly as a result of historical conditions, it has followed that various authorities have in this country the guidance and control of education, with the usual result of want of unity of aim, of lack of correlation of means, and in some cases of overlapping and waste of the means of higher education.

In the second place, while much has been done since the advent of compulsory elementary education to better the means of education and to increase the facilities for the higher instruction of the youth of the country, there is a widespread belief that all the hopes held out by the early advocates of universal compulsory education have not been realised, and that our Primary Schools in large measure have failed to turn out the type of citizen which a State such as ours requires for her after-service.

Universal education has not proved a panacea for all the social evils of the Commonwealth, and while it must be admitted that much good has resulted from the adoption of universal and compulsory education, yet at the same time certain evils have followed in its train.

Since the institution of universal education, it may be argued that the children of the nation have received a better training in the use of the more mechanical arts of reading, writing, and arithmetic, but the tendency has been to look upon the acquisition of these arts as *ends in themselves*, rather than as mere instruments for the further extension and development of knowledge and practice, and hence our Primary School system, to a large extent, has failed to cultivate the imagination of the child, and has also failed to train the reason and to develop initiative on the part of the pupil. There has been more instruction, it has been said, during the last thirty years, but less education; for the process of education consists in the building up within the child's mind of permanent and stable systems of ideas which shall hereafter function in the attainment and realisation of the various ends of life. Now, our school practice is still largely dominated by the old conception that mere memory knowledge is all-important, and as a consequence much of the so-called knowledge acquired during the school period is found valueless in after life to realise any definite purpose, for it is only in so far as the knowledge acquired has been systematised that it can afterwards be turned to use in the furtherance of the aims of adult life.

From this it follows that, since much of the knowledge acquired during the school period has no bearing on the real and practical needs of life, the Primary School in many cases fails to create any permanent or real interest in the works either of nature or of society.

But a much more serious charge is laid at times against our Primary School system. It is contended that during the past thirty years it has done little to raise the moral tone of the community, and it has done still less to develop that sense of civic and national responsibility without which the moral and social progress of a nation is impossible. Our huge city schools are manufactories rather than educational institutions—places where yearly a certain number of the youth of the country are turned out able to some extent to make use of the mechanical arts of reading and writing, and with a smattering of many branches of knowledge, but with little or no training for the moral and civic responsibilities of life. This is evident, it is urged, if we consider how little the school does to counteract and to supplant the evil influences of a bad home or social environment. What truth there may be in these charges and what must be done to remedy this state of matters will be discussed when we consider later the existing Elementary School system. Here it is sufficient to point out that one of the causes at work to-day tending to arouse a renewed interest in educational problems is the feeling now beginning to find expression that the kind of universal elementary education provided somehow or other fails, and has failed, to produce all that was in the beginning expected of it—that it has in the past been too much divorced from the real interests of life, and that it must be remodelled if it is to fit the individual to perform his duty to society.

A third fault often found with our existing school system is that in the case of the majority of the children the process of education stops at too early an age. The belief is slowly spreading that if we are to educate thoroughly the children of the nation so as to fit them to perform efficiently the after duties of life, something of a more systematic character than has as yet been done is required, in order to carry on and to extend the education of the child after the Elementary school stage has been passed. For it is evident that during the Primary School period all that can be expected in the case of the larger number of children is that the school should lay a sound basis in the knowledge of the elementary arts necessary for all social intercourse, and for the realisation of the simpler needs of life. A beginning may be made, during this period, in the formation and establishment of systems of knowledge which have for their aim the realisation of the more complex theoretical and practical interests of after life, but unless these are furthered and extended in the years in which the boy is passing from youth to manhood, then as a consequence much of what has been acquired during the early period fails to be of use either to the individual or to society.

Again, it is surely unwise to give no heed to the systematic education of the majority of the children during the years when they are most susceptible to moral and social influences, and to leave the moral and social education of the youth during the adolescent period to the unregulated and uncertain forces of society.

Lastly, in this connection it is economically wasteful for the nation to spend largely in laying the mere foundations of knowledge, and then to adopt the policy of non-interference, and to leave to the individual parent the right of determining whether the foundation so laid shall be further utilised or not.

A fourth criticism urged against our educational system is that in the past we have paid too little attention to the technical education of those destined in after life to become the leaders of industry and the captains of commerce. Our Higher School system has been too predominantly of one type—it has taken too narrow a view of the higher services required by the State of its members, and our educational system has not been so organised as to maintain and farther the economic efficiency of the State. For it may be contended that the economic efficiency of the individual and of the nation is fundamental in the sense that without this, the attainment of the other goods of life can not or can be only imperfectly realised, and it is obvious that according to the measure in which the economic welfare of the individual and of the State is secured, in like measure is secured the opportunity for the development and realisation of the other aims of the individual and of the nation.

Thus the present unrest as regards our educational affairs may be largely traced to the four causes enumerated. We have begun to realise that our educational system lacks definiteness of aim, and that its various parts are badly co-ordinated; that, in short, we do not as yet possess a national system of education which ministers to and subserves the life of the State as a whole. We are further beginning to perceive that the provision of the means of higher education is too important a matter to be left to the care of the private individual, and that education must be the concern of the whole body of the people. Hence it has been said that on the creation of a national system of education, fitted to meet the needs of the modern State, depends largely the future of Britain as a nation.

Again, all that was hoped for as the result of universal compulsory education has not been realised, and the feeling is growing that there is something defective in the aims of our Primary School system, and that it fails, and has failed, to develop in the individual the moral and social qualities required by a State such as ours, which is becoming increasingly democratic in character. Further, we are learning, partly through experience, partly from the example of other countries, that the period during which our children must be under the regulated control of the school and of society must be lengthened, if we are to realise the final aim of all education, which is to enable the individual on the intellectual side to apply the knowledge gained to the furtherance and extension of the various purposes of life, and on the moral side to enable him to use his freedom rightly.

Lastly, as a nation, we are beginning to discover that without the better technical training of our workmen, and especially of those to whom in after-life will be entrusted the control and direction of our industries and commerce, we are likely to fall behind the other advanced nations in the race for economic supremacy.

But, in addition to these negative forces at work, tending to produce dissatisfaction with our educational position, the opinion is growing stronger and clearer that the education, physical, intellectual, and moral, of the children of the nation is a matter of supreme importance for the future well-being and the future supremacy of the nation, and that it is the duty of the State to see that the opportunity is furnished to each individual to realise to the full all the potentialities of his nature which make for good, so that he may be enabled to render that service to the community for which by nature he is best fitted. Compulsory elementary education is but one stage in the process. We must, as a nation, at least see that no insuperable obstacles are placed in the path of those who have the requisite ability and desire to advance farther in the development of their powers. Moreover, if need be, we must, in the words of Rousseau, compel those who from various causes are unwilling to realise themselves, to attain their full freedom.

This demand for the better and fuller education of the children of the nation is motived partly by the growing conviction that the freedom, political, civil, and religious, which we as a nation enjoy, can only be maintained, furthered, and strengthened in so far as we have educated our children rightly to understand and rightly to use this freedom to which they are heirs. Democracy, as a form of government and as a power for good, is only possible when the mass of the people have been wisely and fully educated, so that they are enabled to take an intelligent and comprehensive interest in all that pertains to the good and future welfare of the State. A democracy of ill or partially educated people sooner or later becomes an ochlocracy,[2] ruled not by the best, but by those who can work upon the self-interest of the badly or one-sidedly educated. A true democracy is in fact ever aristocratic, in the original sense of that term. A false democracy ever tends to become ochlocratic, and the only safeguard against such a state of conditions arising in a country where representative government exists is the spread of higher education, and the inculcation of a right conception of the nature and functions of the State and of the duties of citizenship.

But further, the demand for increased facilities for higher and technical education is motived largely by the conviction that in the education of our children we must in the future more than we have done in the past take means to secure the fitness of the individual to perform efficiently some specific function in the economic organisation of society. And the demand proceeds, not from any desire to narrow down the aims of education, to place it on a purely utilitarian basis, but from the belief that the securing of the physical and economic efficiency of the individual is of fundamental and primary importance both for his own welfare and the well-being and progress of the State, and that in proportion as we secure the higher economic efficiency of a larger and larger number of the people we also secure the essential condition for the development and extension of those other goods of life which can be attained by the majority of a nation only after a certain measure of economic prosperity and economic security is assured.

The social evils of our own or of any time cannot, of course, be removed by any one remedy, but an education which endeavours to secure that each individual shall have the opportunity to develop himself and to fit himself for the after performance of the service for which by nature he is suited may do much to mitigate the evils incident upon the industrial organisation of society. If this end is to be realised, then three things at least are necessary. We must seek by some means or other to check the large number of our boys and girls who, after leaving the Primary School, drift year by year, either through the ignorance or the cupidity or the poverty of their parents, into the ranks of untrained labour, and who in the course of two or three years go to swell the ranks of the unskilled, casual workers, and become in many cases, in the course of time, the unemployed and the unemployable. In the second place, we must endeavour to secure the better technical training of the youth during their years of apprenticeship, and so tend to raise the general efficiency of the workers of the nation whatever the nature—manual or mental—of their employment. In the third place, we must endeavour, by means of our system of education, to increase the mobility of labour. In the modern State, where changes in the industrial organisation are frequent, the worker who can most easily adapt himself to changing circumstances is best assured of constant employment, and a great part of the social evils of our time may be traced to this want of mobility on the part of a large number of our workers.

The mobility of labour is of course always determined within certain limits, but much may and could be done by pursuing from the beginning a right method in educating the child to develop its power of self-adaptation to the needs of a changing environment.

If these results are to be attained, then we shall have, as a nation, to make clear to ourselves the real meaning and purpose of education; we shall have to make explicit the nature of the ends which we desire to secure as the result of our educational efforts, and we shall have to organise our educational agencies so that the ends desired shall be secured.

Let us now consider the question of the meaning, purpose, and ends of education.

FOOTNOTES:

[1] *National Education and National Life*, p. 1.

[2] *Ochlos*, a mob.

CHAPTER II

THE MEANING AND PROCESS OF EDUCATION

"Of all the animals with which the globe is peopled, there is none towards whom nature seems, at first sight, to have exercised more cruelty than towards man, in the numberless wants and necessities with which she has loaded him, and in the slender means which she affords to the relieving of these necessities. In other creatures these two particulars generally compensate each other. If we consider the lion as a voracious and carnivorous animal, we shall easily discover him to be very necessitous, but if we turn our eye to his make and temper, his agility, his courage, his arms, and his force, we shall find that his advantages hold proportion with his wants.... In man alone this unnatural conjunction of infirmity and of necessity may be observed in the greatest perfection. Not only the food which is required for his sustenance flies his search and approach, or at least requires his labour to be produced, but he must be possessed of clothes and lodging to defend him against the injuries of the weather: though to consider him only in himself, he is provided neither with arms, nor force, nor other natural abilities which are in any degree answerable to so many 'necessities.' 'Tis by society alone he is able to supply his defects and raise himself up to an equality with his fellow-creatures, and even acquires a superiority over them."[3] In these terms Hume draws the distinction between man and the animals, and if, for the term Society, we substitute the word Education, then we shall more truly describe the means by which man overcomes his natural infirmities and meets his necessities.

But we have to ask, Wherein does man differ from the animals? what power or faculty does he possess over and above those possessed by himself and the animals in common? and how does it happen that as his wants and needs increase and multiply the means to satisfy them also tend to increase? Now, the animal is guided wholly or mainly by instinct. In the case of many animals the whole conduct of their life from birth to death is governed by this means. In the case, indeed, of some of the higher animals, there is a limited power of modifying this government by instinct through the experience acquired during the lifetime of the individual. But man alone possesses the power or faculty of reason. And it is through the possession of this power that he alone of all creatures can be educated; it is the possession of this power which places him above the rest of creation, and it is in the possession of this power that the possibility of his greatness, and also of his baseness, lies. Now, an instinct may be defined as an inborn and inherited system of means for the attainment of a definite end of such a nature that once the appropriate external stimulus is applied the system tends to work itself out in an automatic manner until the end is attained, and independently of any control exercised by the individual. The working out of such an action may be accompanied by consciousness, but the power of memory would only be valuable in so far as the instinct was imperfect, and in so far as the better attainment of the end was fostered by direct individual experience. Thus the greater the range of instinct the less the scope of and the less the need for education—*i.e.*, for acquiring experiences that will function in rendering more efficient future action; and conversely, the less the range of instinct the greater the need for education, for acquiring experiences that may function in the guidance and direction of future action.

Now, in man the range of instinct is small. In fact, it is questionable whether in the strict usage of the term he possesses any one perfect instinct. But to overcome this weakness of his nature he possesses the power or faculty of reason, and this consists in the ability to self-find, to self-adapt, and to self-establish systems of means for the attainment of definite ends. "Man's splendid power of learning through experience and of applying the contents of his memory to forecast and mould the future is his peculiar glory. It is this which distinguishes him from and raises him above all other animals. This it is that makes him man. This it is that has enabled him to conquer the whole world and to adapt himself to a million conditions of life."[4] This it is that also makes possible the education of the child, and raises the hope that by a truer and deeper conception of the process of education we shall be enabled to mould the character of the children to worthy ends.

But although man is pre-eminently the rational animal, yet reason only operates, and can only operate, in so far as it is called into activity by the need of satisfying some inborn or acquired desire. That is, man possesses not only reason, but also certain instinctive tendencies to action. In early life, the instincts of curiosity, of imitation, of emulation, and the various forms of the play instinct are ever inciting the child to action, and ever evoking his reason-activity to acquire new experiences which shall function in the more efficient performance of future action. At a later stage other instinctive tendencies make their appearance, as *e.g.* the parental instinct, and serve as motives for the further acquisition of new experiences—for the establishment of other systems of means for the attainment of desired ends. But as the child passes from infancy to youth and manhood, these instinctive tendencies, although ever present, alter their character, and acquired ends or interests become the motives of actions. But these acquired ends or interests are not something created out of nothing: they are grafted upon and arise out of the innate and inherited instinctive tendencies of man's nature. Thus, *e.g.*, the instinct of mere self-preservation may pass into the desire to attain a certain standard of life, or to maintain a certain social status; the instinct of curiosity into the desire to find out and to systematise knowledge for its own sake. But for the realisation of these instinctive ends, whether in their crude or acquired forms, the finding and the establishment of systems of means in every case is necessary, and in order that they may be realised man must acquire the requisite capacities for action. In the case of the animal the instinct or impulse to action is inherited, but the capacity for action is also inborn or innate. Man possesses all the innate ends or interests which the animal possesses. Moreover, upon these innate ends or interests can be grafted ends or interests innumerable and varied in character, but in order that they may be satisfied he must through the evoking into activity of reason find and adapt means for their attainment. Thus the general nature of our conscious human life is that throughout we are striving to attain ends of a more or less explicit nature, and endeavouring to find out and to establish means for their attainment. Whether in the performance of some simple, practical act, or in trying to observe accurately what is presented to us through the senses, or in endeavouring to realise imaginatively something not directly presented to the senses, or in performing an abstract process of thought, the activity of reason in its formal aspect is ever one and the same. Hence in education we have not to do with the development of many powers or faculties but with the development or the evolution of the one power or faculty of reason, and the process of development in its general nature is always the same in kind —viz., the process of systematically building up knowledge which shall function in the future determination of conduct. What varies in each case, at each stage of development, is the nature of the material which goes to form this or that system, and the character of the identity or link of connection which binds part to part within any given system. A system of knowledge may be built up of perceptual elements, of ideas derived directly through the medium of the senses. Of such a character are the systems of knowledge possessed by the artist and the musician. Again, a system of knowledge may be composed wholly or mainly of images—of remembered ideas, so altered and so modified as to form and fit into a new whole. Lastly, the elements which go to form the component parts of the system may be of a conceptual character. Thus we may select the number aspect of things for consideration and treatment, and so build up and establish within the mind of the child a number system. But in each and every case the power at work is the activity of reason, and the end ever in view in the selection and in the formation of the system is the satisfaction of some end or interest desired either for its own sake or as a means to some further and remoter end.

Further, a system of knowledge may differ not only in the nature of the materials of which it is composed, but also in the mode of its formation; *i.e.*, the nature of the identity which binds part to part within the system may vary in character. Now it is upon the nature of the systems which we ultimately form in the mind of the child and upon the method which we pursue in our process of system or knowledge making that the resultant character of our education depends.

A system of knowledge may be related as regards its parts by some qualitative or quantitative bond of identity. All sciences of mere classification are formed in this way, and the formation of such systems is in some cases a necessary preliminary to the evolution of the higher forms of system. But the important point to note is that all such systems are valuable only as a means to the further recognition, the further classification, of similar instances. An individual whose mind was wholly formed in this way might be compared to a well-arranged museum, where everything is classified and arranged on the basis of qualitative identity. But manifestly this mere arranging and classifying of knowledge has only a limited value. Such systems can never be used as means for the realisation of any practical need of life, can never by themselves lead us to intrinsically connected knowledge.

A second and higher form of system is established whenever the bond of connection between part and part is an identity of function or of law. All language systems are of this nature, and the more highly synthetic the language the more intrinsic the connection there is between the parts of the system. Further, it should be noted that systems of this character can be used for the attainment of other ends than those of mere recognition and classification. They, of course, can be used as instruments of intercourse, of culture, and of commerce. But they may further be utilised in education in the training of the pupil to self-apply a system of knowledge to the solution of relatively new problems, and it is for this reason mainly that the ancient languages possess their value as educational instruments.

Lastly, systems of knowledge may be formed in which the inter-relation of part to part within the system is that of identity of cause and effect. In the establishment of scientific knowledge the aim is to show the causal inter-relation of part to part within a systematic whole or unity. Hence also, as in the case of language systems, systems of this nature are capable of being used to train the pupil to self-apply knowledge in the solution of practical and theoretical problems, and in the realising of the practical ends of life. Once again it must be noted that in the establishment of the various systems of knowledge the one activity ever present is that of reason seeking ever to connect part to part in order that some end or interest may be attained. Moreover, we may misuse the power of reason, and employ it in the attainment of ends which are valueless in the sense that they further no real interest or end in life. This is done whenever knowledge is crammed, whenever the bond of connection between one part of knowledge and the other is extrinsic, and whenever facts are connected and remembered by bonds of a more or less accidental or factitious nature. And since such knowledge can further no direct interest or end in life, its acquisition must, as a rule, be motived by some strong indirect interest. As a consequence, whenever the indirect interest, whatever its nature may be,—the fear of punishment, or the passing of an examination,—ceases to operate, then the desire for further acquisition also ceases. Hence it follows that the establishment of any such system is of comparatively little value. It may pave the way at a later period for the formation of a system of intrinsically connected knowledge, but as a general rule such systems, because they cannot be used, tend soon to drop out of mind, and to be of no further consequence in the determination of conduct. But further, this misuse of reason, this inciting of the mind to memorise facts unrelated except by their mere accidental time or space relations, will if persisted in tend to render the individual dull, stupid, and unimaginative.

The systems of knowledge, then, of most value are those which establish intrinsic connections between part and part; for it is only by means of systems of this character that action can be determined and knowledge extended. In this sense we may agree with Herbert Spencer[5] that science or systematised knowledge is of chiefest value both for the guidance of conduct and for the discipline of mind. At the same time we must not fall into the Spencerian error of identifying science "with the study of surrounding phenomena," and in making the antithesis between science and linguistic studies one between dealing with real things on the one hand, and mere words on the other.

Further, since the establishment of a system of means is always through the self-finding and the self-forming of the system, this furnishes the key to the only sound method of education—viz., that the child must be trained in the self-discovering and the self-connecting of knowledge. This does not mean that the method should be heuristic in Rousseau's sense, that the child should be told nothing, but be left to rediscover all knowledge for himself. But it does mean that in the imparting of the garnered experience of the race the child must be trained in the methods by which the race has slowly and gradually built up a knowledge of the means necessary for the realisation of the many and complex ends of civilised life.

Before passing on to consider the ends at which we should aim in the education of the child, it may be well briefly to summarise the conclusions reached.

1. Man is distinguished from the rest of creation by the possession of reason: the animal life is mainly or wholly guided by instinct.

2. Man like the animals possesses instincts or instinctive tendencies, but for their realisation he must seek out and establish systems of means for their attainment. Bereft of these instinctive tendencies of his nature, man would have no incentive to acquire experiences for the more efficient guidance of his future conduct.

3. In the course of the development and extension of experience there gradually becomes grafted upon these innate instincts, interests or ends of an acquired nature, and one of the main functions of education is to create, foster, and establish on a permanent and stable basis, interests of ethical and social worth.

4. The power of reason is no occult power: it is simply the capacity for finding and establishing systems of means for the attainment of ends; or it may be defined as the power of acquiring experience and of self-applying this experience in the future guidance of conduct.

5. The evolution of intelligence in man is the evolution of this reason-activity to the attainment of new and more complex theoretical and practical ends or interests. At an early stage the systems of knowledge established are for the attainment of the relatively simple needs of life, and are composed of perceptual and imagined elements. At a later stage the systems formed may be of the most complex nature, and are composed of conceptual elements.

6. Man is the only being capable of education in the strict usage of the term. He alone must acquire the means for the realisation of the various desired ends of life.

7. The process of education is a process which, utilising as motives to acquirement the instinctive tendencies of the child's nature, seeks to establish systems of means for their realisation, and upon these innate or inborn instincts to graft acquired ends or interests which shall hereafter function in the attainment of ends of economic, ethical, and social worth.

8. The only truly educative method is the method which trains the pupil to find, establish, and apply systems of knowledge in the attainment of ends of felt value.

FOOTNOTES:

[3] Hume's *Treatise of Human Nature*, Bk. III. part ii. sec. 2.

[4] *Principles of Heredity*, by G. Archdall Reid, p. 235.

[5] Cf. Herbert Spencer, *Education*, especially chap. i.

CHAPTER III

THE END OF EDUCATION

We have seen that the process of education is the process of acquiring and organising experiences that will function in the determination of future conduct and ensure the more efficient performance of future action; or we may say that the process is one by which means are gradually established and fixed in the mind for the attainment of ends of value for the realisation of the varied and complex interests of life.

Now, this acquisition and organisation of experience is never entirely "left to the blind control of inherited impulse," nor is the child wholly left to gather and organise his experiences upon the incentive of any innate or acquired interest that may for the time engage his will. The various agencies of society—the home, the school, the shop and yard—are ever constantly seeking to establish such or such systems of ideas, and to prevent the formation of other systems. Hence it follows that education is not a mere natural process—not a process of acquiring experience in response to the demands of this or that natural need, but that it is a regulated process, controlled with the view of finally leading the child to acquire certain experiences, to organise certain systems of means for the attainment of such or such ends.

Moreover, at various periods in history, the end or ends of education, the kinds of experience thought necessary and valuable for the child to acquire have varied, and still vary, and must vary according to the nature of the civilisation into which the child is born and to which his education must somehow or other adjust him; *i.e.*, there is no one type of experience, no one kind of education, which is equally suited to meet the needs of the child born in a modern industrial State and the child whose education must fit him hereafter to fulfil his duties as a member of a savage tribe.

Further, in determining the nature of the experiences useful to acquire, we must take into account not only the civilisation to which the child is to be adjusted, but we must also take note of the nature of the services which the given society requires of its adult members. These services vary in character, and there can be no one kind of education which equally fits the individual to perform efficiently any and every service. To postulate this would be to affirm that there is a kind of experience useful for the realisation indifferently of any and every purpose of adult life, and to affirm that a system of knowledge acquired and organised for the attainment of certain definite ends can be used for the furtherance of ends different in character and having no intrinsic connection with each other. Further, to assert that there is one type of education equally suited to train and to develop the reason-activity of the individual in every direction is to neglect the fact that individuals differ in innate capacity. These differences are due in part to differences in the extent and character of the receptive powers of individuals, and are to be traced, probably, to differences in the size and constitution of the sensory areas of the brain, and are due also in part to inborn differences in the capacity for acquiring and utilising experiences. As a consequence of these differences one individual will acquire and organise certain kinds of experience more readily than others.

But not only have the ends sought to be realised through the educational agencies of society varied in the past—not only do we find that the ideals at present vary in character according to the stage of civilisation which the particular country has reached—we also find that the agencies of society determining the character and end of education also vary. For in the discussion of the ends sought to be attained by means of education, we must remember that these are not determined by the teacher, but by "the adult portion of the Community organised in the forms of the Family, the State, the Church, and various miscellaneous associations"[6] desirous of promoting the welfare of the community. At one time the Church largely determined the character and ends of education, but the tendency at the present time is for the State to control more and more the education of the rising generation. In some countries the entire control of all forms of education, primary, secondary, and technical, has come under the guidance of the State, and in our own country elementary education is now largely under the control of the State authorities, and the other forms of education tend increasingly to come under this control. Not only is this so, but the period during which the State exercises its control over the education of the child is gradually being lengthened.

Many causes are at work tending to produce these results in the first place, it is being clearly realised that there can be no thorough-going co-ordination of the various grades of instruction until all the agencies of education in each area are placed under one authority acting under the guidance of some central body responsible for the organisation and direction of the education of the district as a whole. Further, there can be no satisfactory settlement of the problem as to what particular function each distinct type of Higher School shall perform until the whole means of education are under one determining authority.

In the second place, the higher education of the children of the nation is too important a matter to be left entirely to the care of the private individual, and its cost is too great in many cases to be wholly borne by each individual parent. But this provision, organisation, and control of the means of higher education by the State does not necessarily imply that it should be free— that the whole burden should be laid on the shoulders of the general taxpayer. Yet unless means are provided by which the poor but clever boy can realise himself, then there is so much loss to the community.

In the third place, the organisation of all forms of education and the more extended provision of higher and especially of technical training is necessary, if for no other reason than as a means of economic protection and economic security.

Lastly, the better organisation of our educational agencies is necessary as a means of securing a democracy capable of understanding the meaning of moral and civic freedom and of using this rightly.

But while the concrete nature of the ends to which our educational efforts are directed may vary in accordance with the needs of a changing and progressive civilisation, nevertheless the general nature of the ends sought to be attained by the education of the children of a nation is permanent and unchangeable. That is, we have to recognise a universal as well as a particular element in our educational ideals. Now, the universal aim of all education is, or rather should be, to correlate the child with the civilisation of his time; to lead him to acquire those experiences which will in after-life enable him to perform ably and rightly his duties as a worker, as a citizen, and as a member of an ethical and spiritual community organised for the securing of the well-being of the individual. And the higher the civilisation, the more difficult, the more complex, and the more lengthened must be this process of acquiring experiences necessary to fit the individual to his environment. Hence, whatever the particular nature of the environment may be, the aim of education must be the fitting of the individual to his natural and social environments. Hence also any organisation of the means of education must have as its threefold object the securing of the physical efficiency, of the economic efficiency, and the ethical efficiency of the rising generation. In short, as Mr. Bagley[7] puts it, the securing of the social efficiency of the individual must be the ultimate aim of all education. To be socially efficient implies that as the result of the process of education certain experiences, and the power of applying them, have been acquired by each individual, so that by this means he is enabled to perform some particular social service for the community of a directly or indirectly economic nature. For if, as the result of the educative process, we establish systems of means for the realisation of ends which have no social value, then so far we have failed to make the individual socially efficient. "The youth we would train has little time to spare; he owes but the first fifteen or sixteen years of his life to his tutor, the remainder is due to action. Let us employ this short time in necessary instruction. Away with your crabbed, logical subtleties; they are abuses, things by which our lives can never be made better."[8] In these words Montaigne writes against the false ideal that the mere accumulation of knowledge apart from any purpose it may serve in enabling us better to understand either the world of nature or of history should be the aim of education, and throughout all education we must ever keep in mind that knowledge acquired must be capable of being used and applied for the realisation of some social purpose, otherwise it is so much useless lumber, to the individual a burden, soon dropped, to society valueless, since it can maintain and further no real interest of the community.

But to be socially efficient implies not merely that the individual should be fitted to perform some service economically useful to the community, it further implies that as the result of the process of education there should have been acquired certain capacities of action which restrain him from unduly interfering with the freedom of others. He must acquire certain experiences which restrain him from hindering the full and free development of others; he must be trained to use his freedom rightly, to acquire those capacities for action which fit him to take his place in the moral cosmos of his time and generation. Further, as Mr. Bagley also points out, to be socially efficient implies in addition that the individual should contribute something further to the advancement of the civilisation into which he is born, and thus pass on to his successors an increasing heritage.

The threefold aim of all education, then, is to secure the physical, the economic, and the ethical efficiency of the future members of the community; and our educational agencies must throughout keep this threefold aspect in view.

To secure the physical efficiency of the child is necessary, in the first place, because a strong, healthy, vigorous body is a good in itself, apart from the fact that without sound health the other ends of life cannot, or can be only imperfectly realised. It is an erroneous point of view to maintain that many men have done good intellectual work in spite of physical ill-health, and even in cases where there was present some physical defect. The real thing to keep in mind is that these individuals do not represent the average, and that for the normal individual weak health or the presence of physical defect lessens his intellectual and moral vigour. We can, in the light of modern psychology, no longer regard mind and body as separate entities having a development independent of each other, but must regard them as conditioning and conditioned by each other.

In the second place, the care of the physical health of the child is important, because any impairment or defect in the sense organs—the avenues of experience—implies a corresponding defect or want in mental growth, and as a consequence tends to render the individual economically and socially less efficient in after-life.

In the third place, and this truth is being gradually put into practice in the education of the weak-minded and of the physically defective, sound physical health is one of the conditions of right moral activity. This truth Rousseau emphasised when he declared: "that the weaker the body, the more it commands; the stronger it is, the better it obeys. All the sensual passions find lodgment in effeminate bodies, and the less they are satisfied the more irritable they become. The body must needs be vigorous to obey the soul: a good servant ought to be robust."

We shall inquire further into this question when we come to treat of the physical education of the child, but what we wish to point out is that one aim of all our educational efforts must be to secure the physical efficiency of the rising generation, on the grounds that sound physical health is a good in itself; is a means to the securing of the economic efficiency of the individual and of society; and is a condition of securing the ethical efficiency of the individual.

In the second place, the securing of the economic efficiency of the individual must be one of the aims of our educational efforts. This does not imply that our educational curriculum should be based on purely utilitarian lines, and that all subjects whose utilitarian value is not immediately apparent should be banished from the schoolroom. But it does imply that whether in the education of the professional man or of the industrial worker all instruction either directly or indirectly must have as its final result the efficiency of the individual as a worker. An education which fits the individual to use his leisure rightly may have as much effect in increasing the productive powers of the individual as that which looks more narrowly to his technical training. Further, we must remember that the larger number by far of the children of the modern State must in after-life become industrial workers, and that any system of education which neglects this fact, which makes no provision for the technical training of the children of the working classes, and has no adequate system of selecting and training those who by innate capacity are fitted to become the leaders in industry, is a system not in harmony with the characteristics of modern life, and that unless this economic efficiency is secured, then the opportunity for the development of the other ends of life cannot be secured.

Lastly, the securing of the ethical efficiency of the future members of the State must be one of our ultimate aims. The ethical aim of education may be said to be the supreme end, in the sense that it is the essential condition for the security, the stability, and the progress of society; and also from the fact that the ethical spirit of doing the work for the sake of the work should permeate all education.

In concluding this chapter what needs to be emphasised is that while the process of education remains ever the same, ever consists in acquiring and organising experience, in and through the working of reason incited to activity by the need of satisfying some natural or acquired interest, in order that future action may be rendered more efficient, and whilst the general nature of the ends to be attained may be said to be permanent and unchangeable, yet the particular and concrete ends at which we should aim in the education of our children is a practical question which every nation has, from time to time, to ask and answer afresh in the light of her national ideals and in view of her national aspirations. Nay, further, it is a question which with every necessary change in her internal organisation, and with every fundamental alteration in her relation to her external neighbours, has to be asked and answered anew by each and every State desirous of retaining her place amongst the nations of the world and of securing the welfare and happiness of her individual members. It is mainly because we as a nation have not realised this truth that our educational organisation has, neither in the explicitness and clearness of its aims, nor in the distinction, gradation, and co-ordination of its means, attained the same thoroughness and self-consistency as that possessed by the educational systems of some of our Continental neighbours.

FOOTNOTES:

[6] Cf. Professor Findlay, *Journal of Education* (Sept. 1899), also "*Principles of Class Teaching,*" p. 2.

[7] Cf. *The Educative Process*, chap. iii., esp. pp. 59, 60 (Macmillan).

[8] Montaigne, *The Education of Children*, L. E. Rector, Ph.D. (*International Education Series*), Appleton, New York.

CHAPTER IV

THE RELATION OF THE STATE TO EDUCATION—THE PROVISION OF EDUCATION

The end of education is, as we have seen, the securing of the future social efficiency of the rising generation, and the method in every case is through the evoking of the reason-activity of the individual to organise and establish in the minds of the young and immature, systems of ideas which will hereafter function as means in the attainment of ends of definite social worth.

The question now arises as to whether the provision and organisation of the agencies of education may be safely left to the care and self-interest of the individual parent, or whether on principle such provision is a duty which devolves upon the State.

The principle of the State provision of the means of elementary education has now practically been admitted, and whether wisely or unwisely, the larger part by far of the cost of this provision now falls upon the shoulders of the general and local taxpayer. *E.g.*, in England in 1902 there were six hundred and thirty-three thousand fee-paying children in the Public Elementary Schools, and over five millions receiving their education free. [9] Further, by the Education Act (England) of 1902 and by the Education and Local Taxation Account (Scotland) Act of the same year the principle of the State aid for the provision of the means of secondary and technical education may be said also practically to have been recognised. By the former Act certain Imperial funds derived from the income on Probate and Licence duties were handed over to the Councils of counties and boroughs for expenditure on the provision of the means of education other than elementary, and at the same time these bodies were empowered, if they thought it necessary, to impose a limited rate for the same purpose. In Scotland at the same time a certain part of Scotland's share of the "whisky" money was set aside for the provision of secondary education in urban and rural districts, and Secondary Education Committees were appointed in the counties and principal boroughs charged with the allocation of the funds towards the aid and increase of the provision of higher education in their respective districts.

But while this has been done, the question as to whether and to what extent the State should undertake the provision of the means of higher education is still one on which there is no general agreement. If it is the duty of the State to see that the provision of the means of education, elementary, secondary, technical, and university, is adequate to the attainment of the end of securing the future social efficiency of all the members of the community, then it must be admitted that the means at present provided for this purpose are totally inadequate, and that the method followed in furnishing this provision is not of a kind to ensure that the funds granted are spent in the manner best calculated to extend the agencies and to increase the efficiency of the higher education of the children of the nation. This latter objection applies more especially in the case of Scotland. In that country certain nominated bodies who are responsible only to themselves and to the Scotch Education Department are entrusted with the expenditure of the monies received for the extension of the means of higher education, and since these bodies stand in no intimate connection with the representative bodies entrusted with the control of elementary education, no efficient co-ordination of the two grades of education is possible. Further, in some cases sectional interests rather than the educational interests of the district as a whole are the main motives at work in determining the distribution of the funds amongst the various bodies claiming to participate in its benefits. The uncertainty of the amount of income available for this purpose, and the limitation in England of the power of rating, might also be urged in objection to this peculiarly English method of providing the means for the higher education of the youth of the country.

Similar reasons to those urged prior to 1870 in favour of the State provision of elementary education may be urged in favour of the extension of the principle to higher education. These reasons are nowhere more clearly stated than in the writings of John Stuart Mill.

In discussing the functions of government, Mill lays down that education is one of those things which it is admissible on principle that a Government should provide for the people, and although in adducing the reasons for the

State undertaking this duty he is concerned mainly with the provision of the means of elementary education, yet looking to the altered social conditions of our own time, and taking into account the difference in the economic relations which exist now between Great Britain and her Continental rivals, the arguments advanced by Mill are no less applicable now to the extension of the principle of State provision. Let us consider these arguments.

In the first place, Mill declares that there are "certain primary elements and means of knowledge that all human beings born into the community must acquire during childhood." If their parents have the power of obtaining for them this instruction and fail to do so, they commit a double breach of duty. The child grows up an imperfect being, socially inefficient, and members of the community are liable to suffer seriously from the consequences of this ignorance and want of education in their fellow-citizens.

In the second place, Mill urges that unlike that the giving of other forms of help, the provision of education is not one of the things in which the tender of help perpetuates the state of things which renders help necessary. Instruction strengthens and enlarges the active faculties; its effect is favourable to the growth of the spirit of independence—it is help towards doing without help.

In the third place, he declares that the question of the provision of elementary education is not one between its provision by the Government on the one hand, and its provision through voluntary agencies on the other. The full cost of the education of the children of the lower working classes in Great Britain as in other countries has never been wholly paid for out of the wages of the labourer, and hence the question lies between the State provision of education and its provision by certain charitable agencies. As a rule, when provided by the latter, it is both inefficient in quantity and poor in quality.

Lastly, Mill lays down that in the matter of education the intervention of Government is necessary, because neither the interest nor the judgment of the consumer is a sufficient security for the goodness of the commodity.

But at the same time he strenuously insists that there should be no monopoly of education by the State. It is not desirable, he declares, that a government should have complete control over the education of the people.

To possess such a control and actually to exert it would be despotic. The State may, however, require that all its people shall have received a certain measure of education, but it may not prescribe from whom or where they may obtain it.

At the present day, and under the changed economic conditions which now prevail, it can no longer be asserted that the imparting of the mere elements of knowledge is adequate either to secure the future social efficiency of the children of the lower classes of society or that such a modicum of instruction as is provided by our Elementary Schools is sufficient to protect the community from the ignorance of its ill educated and badly trained members. The "hooliganism" of many of our large cities is due to our system of half educating, half training the children of the slums, of laying too much stress on the acquisition of certain mechanical arts in our Primary Schools and in conceiving them as ends in themselves. Further, our system of primary education fails on its moral side, and this in two ways. It seems unaware of the fact that all moral education is an endeavour to implant in the minds of the young desires that shall impel them hereafter to good rather than to evil, and that this end can only be attained in so far as the natural instinctive tendencies of the child's nature which make for good are cultivated and trained, and in so far as those other instinctive tendencies which make for social destruction are inhibited by having their character altered so as to be directed into channels which make for the social welfare. In the second place, we leave off the education of the children at too early an age. We hand over the children of the poorer classes during the most critical period of their lives to the influences of the streets and of the bad home, counteracted only by the efforts of the slum visitor or the missionary. After furnishing them with the mere instruments of knowledge, we entrust either to them or their parents the liberty of using, misusing, or non-using the instruments provided. Moreover, we do nothing of a systematic nature to instil into the youth of our poorer citizens the fact that they are members of a corporate community and future citizens of a State, and that hereafter they have duties towards that State the performance of which is the only rational ground of their possession of rights as against the State. *E.g.*, in many of our slums we have the best examples of individualism run mad, of the conception that the individual is a law unto his private self, and that all government is something alien, something forced upon the individual from the outside and impinging upon his private will, instead of law being what it really is, an expression of the social conditions under which the welfare of the individual and of society may be attained.

Further, it must be maintained that our present policy in education is economically wasteful. To spend, as we do yearly, larger and larger sums of money on the elementary education of our children, and then, in a large number of cases, to fail to reach the ends of securing either the social efficiency of the individual or the protection of society against the ignorance of its members, is surely, to say the least, unwise. Again, if we really set before us this aim of the social efficiency of the future individual, we must do something to carry on the education of the children of the poorer classes after the Elementary School stage has been passed.

One of the strongest points in the German system of education, as compared and contrasted with our own, is the care which is taken of the higher education of the children of the working classes during the period when it is most important that some control should be exercised over the youth of the country, throughout the time when the boy is most open to temptation, and when the moral forces of society are potent for good and evil in shaping and forming his character. The great majority of the children in a modern State are and must be destined for industrial service; the great majority of the children of the working classes must, at or about the age of fourteen, leave the Primary School and enter upon the learning of some trade. But manifestly at this early stage the larger number are not fitted to guide and control their own lives; and if moral education aims, as it ought to aim, at fitting the individual for freedom, at fitting him to guide and direct his own life in the light of a self-accepted and a self-directed ideal, then some measure of control, of guidance, and of regulation is necessary in the years when the child is passing from youth to manhood. Now, it is this fact, this truth, which the Germans as a nation have realised. They declare that it is neither wise nor prudent nor for the ultimate benefit of the State to leave the vast majority of the youth without guidance, and sometimes even without proper moral control exercised over them during the great formative period of their lives. Nay, further, they believe that a State which neglects its duty here is not doing what it ought to do for the future moral good, for the future economic welfare, and for the future happiness of its individual members. Hence, in several of the German States, the State control over the child does not cease when at fourteen years of age he leaves the Elementary School, but is continued until the age of seventeen; and this is effected by the establishment of compulsory Evening Schools. In particular, by a law which came into force in Berlin on the 1st April 1905, every boy and girl in that city, with certain definitely specified exceptions, must attend at an Evening Continuation School for a minimum of not less than four hours and a maximum of not more than six hours per week. Moreover, this enactment has been rendered necessary not to level up the majority, but to level up the minority. This development is a development for which the voluntary Evening Continuation School prepared the way; and compulsory attendance has become possible on account of the willingness of the German youth to learn, and of his desire to make himself proficient in his particular trade or profession. Further, the school authorities, in this matter of compulsory attendance at an Evening Continuation School, have with them the hearty co-operation of the great body of employers; and the burden of seeing that the pupil attends regularly is not put upon the parent but upon the employer. By these means, and by other agencies of a voluntary character, every care is taken that the Berlin youth shall have the opportunity of finding that employment for which by nature he is best suited, and that thereafter he shall learn thoroughly the particular trade or calling he may enter upon.

Contrast what we do, or rather what we do not do, in this matter of providing higher education for the sons and daughters of the working classes. In our large towns the great majority of our boys and girls leave the Elementary School at or before the age of fourteen. In many cases the instruction given during this period soon passes away, and leaves little permanent result behind. Evening Continuation Schools are indeed provided, but only a small proportion of our youth takes advantage of this means of further instruction. The larger number of the children of the lower working classes drift, for a year or two, into various forms of unskilled employment, chosen in most cases because the immediate pecuniary reward is here greater than in the case of learning a trade; and after spending two or three years in employments which do nothing to educate them, some drift, by accident, into this or that particular trade, while the others remain behind to swell the number of the unskilled. During this period nothing of an organised nature is done to secure the physical efficiency of the youth of our working classes; nothing or almost nothing is done to secure his future industrial efficiency; and, as a consequence, year after year, as a nation, we go on fostering an army of loafers, increasing the ranks of the unskilled workers, and even in our skilled trades adding to the number of those who are mere process workers, at the expense of producing workers acquainted both theoretically and practically with every department of their particular calling. No wonder that the delegates of the brass-workers[10] of Birmingham, contrasting what they have seen in Berlin with what they daily see in their own trade at home and in their own city, bitterly declare that the Berlin youth has from infancy been under better care and training at home, at school, at the works, and in the Army; and consequently, as a man, he is more fitted to be entrusted with the liberty which the Birmingham youth has perhaps from childhood only abused.

Space does not permit me to go at fuller length into this question, but before leaving the particular problem let me put the issue plainly, because it is an issue which we as a nation must soon clearly realise, and must answer in either one or other of two ways. We may go on as at present, insisting that a certain amount of elementary education is compulsory for all, and leaving it a matter for the individual parent and the individual youth to take advantage of the means of higher education provided voluntarily, and as a rule without any great direct cost to them. In this way, trusting to the voluntary agencies at work in society, we may hope that either through enlightened self-interest, or through a higher conception of the duty of the individual to the State, or through a loftier moral ideal becoming prevalent and actual in society, an increasing number of parents will see that the means provided for the higher education of their children are duly taken advantage of, and that the majority of the youth will make it their aim to use these means to secure their physical and industrial efficiency. If we adopt this course, then it must be the duty of the school authorities of the various districts to see that Evening Schools of various types suited to the needs of the various classes of students are duly provided, and that no insurmountable obstacles are placed in the way of those desirous and anxious to take advantage of the means of higher education. Further, it must become the duty of the employers of the country to see that the youth are encouraged in every way to take advantage of instruction designed with the above-named end in view, and moreover the general public must do all in their power to co-operate with and to aid the endeavours of school authorities and employers of labour. In this way, as has been the case in Berlin, the voluntary system of Evening Continuation and Trade Schools may gradually and in time pave the way for the compulsory Evening School. Without doubt this were the better way, if it could be effected and that quickly.

But if in this matter we have delayed too long—if we have allowed our educational policy in the past to be guided by a one-sided and narrow individualism—if for too lengthened a period we have permitted our political action to be determined by the false ideal that, in the matter of providing for and furthering his education as a citizen and as an industrial worker, liberty for each individual consists in allowing him to choose for himself, regardless of whether or not that choice is for his own and the State's ultimate good, then it may be necessary in the immediate future to take steps to remove or remedy this defect in our present educational organisation. For it is necessary—essentially necessary—on various grounds that the education of the boys and girls of our working classes should not cease absolutely at the Elementary School stage,[11] but that, with certain definite and well-considered exceptions, all should continue for several years thereafter to fit themselves for industrial and social service. If this result can be effected by moral means, good and well; if not, legal compulsion must, sooner or later, be resorted to. For it is, as it has always been, a fundamental maxim of political action that the State should and must compel her members to utilise the means by which they may be raised to freedom.

The second line of argument which Mill follows in his advocacy of the State provision of education is that instruction is one of the cases in which the aid given does not foster and re-create the evil which it seeks to remedy. Education which is really such does not tend to enervate but to strengthen the individual. Its effect is favourable to the growth of independence. "It is a help towards doing without help."

On similar grounds, we may urge that it is the duty of the State to see that the means for the higher education of the youth of the country are adequate in quantity and efficient in quality. The better technical training of our workmen is necessary if we are to secure their economic self-sufficiency and fit them to become socially useful as members of a community. One aim therefore underlying any future organisation of education must be to secure the industrial efficiency of the worker and to ensure that the results of science shall be utilised in the furtherance of the arts and industries of life. This can only be effected by the better scientific training, by the more intensive and the more thorough education of those children of the nation who by natural ability and industry are fitted in after-life to guide and control the industries of the country.

Mr. Haldane,[12] during the past few years, in season and out of season, has called the attention of the public of Great Britain to the fact that in the organisation and equipment of their system of technical education Germany is much in advance of this country, and that the German people have thoroughly and practically realised that, if they are to compete successfully with other nations, then one of the aims of their educational system must be to teach the youth how to apply knowledge in the furtherance and advancement of the economic interests of life. With this end in view we have the establishment throughout the German States of numerous schools and colleges having as their chief aim the application of knowledge to the arts and industries. In our own country this branch—this very important branch—of education has been left, for the most part, to the care of private individuals, and although the State has done something in recent years to encourage and develop this side of education, yet much more requires to be done; and, above all, it is desirable that whatever is done in the future should be done in a regular, systematic, and organised manner and with definite aims in view.

But it is not merely in the higher reaches of German education that the industrial aim is kept in view. It pervades and permeates the whole system from the lowest to the highest stages. Even in the Primary School the requirements of practical life are not left out of sight. In school, said a former Prussian Director of Education, "children are to learn how to perform duties, they are to be habituated to work, to gain pleasure in work, and thus become efficient for future industrial pursuits. This has been the aim from the earliest times of Prussian education; and to this day it is plainly understood by all State and local administrative officers, as well as by all teachers and the majority of the parents, that the people's school has more to do than merely teach the vehicles of culture—reading, writing, and arithmetic"—that the chief aim is rather "the preparation of citizens who can and will cheerfully serve their God and their native country as well as themselves."

In the third place, the question of the provision of the means of higher education is not one between its provision on the one hand by means of the Government, and on the other by means of purely voluntary agencies. Higher education, *e.g.*, in Scotland has rarely been provided and paid for at its full cost by the individual parent or by associations of individual parents, but has been maintained, in some cases in a high degree of efficiency, by endowments left for this purpose. These endowments are now in many cases insufficient to meet the demand made for education, and the stream of private benevolence in providing the means of education has either ceased to flow or flows in an irregular and uncertain fashion. Further, the incomes of even the moderately well-to-do of our middle classes are not sufficient to bear the whole cost of the more expensive education required to fit their sons and daughters for the after-service of the community. Hence, just as in Mill's time the question of the provision of elementary education lay between the State provision and the provision by means of charitable agencies, so to-day the problem of the provision of secondary and technical education is between its adequate provision and organisation by the State, and its inadequate, uncertain provision by means of the endowments of the past and by the charitable agencies of the present. Manifestly, in the light of modern conditions, with the economic competition between nation and nation becoming keener and keener, and knowing full well that the future belongs to the nation with the best equipped and the best trained army of industrial workers, we can no longer rest content with any haphazard method of providing the means of higher education: whatever the cost may be, we must realise that the time has come to put our educational house in order and to establish and organise our system of higher education so that it will subserve each and every interest of the State. This can only be effected in so far as the nation as a whole realises the need for the better education of the children, and takes steps to secure that this shall be provided, and that there shall be afforded to each the opportunity of fitting himself by education to put his talents to the best use both for his own individual good and the good of the community. Lastly, as Mill urges, the self-interest of the individual is neither sufficient to ensure that the education will be provided, nor in many cases is his judgment sufficient to ensure the goodness of the education provided by voluntary means.

But, in addition to the reasons urged by Mill for the State provision and control of the means of elementary education, and these reasons are, as we have seen, as urgent and as cogent to-day for the extension of the principle to the provision of the means of secondary and technical education, still further reasons may be advanced.

In the first place, there can be no co-ordination of the different stages of education until all the agencies of instruction in each area or district are placed under one central control. Until this is effected we must have at times overlapping of the agencies of instruction. In some cases there may also be waste of the means of education. In every case there will be a general want of balance between the various parts of the system.

In the second place, one object of any organisation of the means of education should be the selection of the best ability from amongst the children of our Elementary Schools and the further education of this ability at some one or other type of Intermediate or Secondary School. In order that this may be economically and efficiently effected, the instruction of the Elementary School should enable the pupil at a certain age to fit himself into the work of the High School, and our High Schools' system should be so differentiated in type as to furnish not one type of such education but several in accordance with the main classes of service required by the community of its adult members. Manifestly such a co-ordination of the means and such a grading of the agencies of education, if not impossible on the voluntary principle, is at least difficult of complete realisation.

Hence, on the ground that the higher education of the young is necessary for the securing of their after social efficiency, on the ground that it is necessary for the economic and social security of the community, on the ground that aid in higher education is a help towards doing without help and that its provision in many cases cannot be fully met by the voluntary contribution of the individual, we may urge the need for the State's undertaking its adequate and efficient provision.

Further, we must remember that the State must take a "longer" view of the problem of education than is possible for the individual. At best the latter looks but one generation ahead. He is content to secure the education and the future welfare of his children. In the life of the State this is not sufficient. She must look to the needs of the remote future as well as of the immediate present, and hence her educational outlook must be wider and go farther than that of any mere private individual. Lastly, if we understand the true nature and function of the State, we need have no fear that the State should control the education of all the people. What we have to fear on the one side is the bureaucratic control of education, and on the other its control and direction by one class in the interests of itself. The State exists for—the reason of its very being is to secure—the welfare of the individual, and the State approaches its perfection when its organisation is fitted to secure and ensure the widest scope for the full and free development of each individual.

The evil of bureaucracy can be removed only by our representative bodies becoming more effective voices of the social and moral will of the community, just as the evil of class control can only be effectually abolished by the rise and spread of the true democratic spirit, ever seeking that the agencies of the State shall be directed towards the removing of the obstacles which hinder the full realisation of the life of each of its members.

FOOTNOTES:

[9] Cf. Graham Balfour, *Educational System of Great Britain*, p. 27, 2nd ed.

[10] *Brass-workers of Berlin and Birmingham* (King).

[11] "It must not be forgotten that the instruction of the common schools (*Volksschule*), closing with the pupil's fourteenth year, ends too soon, that the period most susceptible to aid, most in need of education, the years from fifteen to twenty ... are now not only allowed to lie perfectly fallow, but to lose and waste what has been so laboriously acquired during the preceding period at school." In the rural parts of Northern Germany efforts are being made to remedy this evil by the institution of schools providing half-year winter courses. Cf. Professor Paulsen's *The German Universities and University Study*, p. 117 (English translation).

[12] Cf. *Education and Empire*.

CHAPTER V

THE RELATION OF THE STATE TO EDUCATION—THE COST OF EDUCATION

But while we may hold that it is the duty of the State to see that the means for the education of the children of the nation is both adequate in extent and efficient in quality, and so organised that it affords opportunities for each to secure the education which is needed to equip him for his after-work in life, it by no means follows as a logical consequence that the whole cost of this provision should be borne by the community in its corporate capacity and that the individual parent should, if he so chooses, be relieved from any direct payment for the education of his children. To assert this would be implicitly to affirm that the education of a man's children is no part of his duty—that it is an obligation which does not fall upon him as an individual, but only as a member of a community, and that so long as he pays willingly the proportion of the cost of education assigned to him by taxes and rates, he has fulfilled his obligation. Education, on such a view, becomes a matter of national concern in which as a private individual the parent has no direct interest. This position carried out to its logical conclusion would imply that the child and his future belong wholly to the State, and it would also involve the establishment of a communal system of education such as is set forth in the *Republic* of Plato. Further, such a position logically leads to the contention that the other necessities of life requisite for securing the social efficiency of the future members of the State should also be provided by the State in its corporate capacity acting as the guardian of the young, and from this we are but a short way from the position that it belongs to the community to superintend the propagation of the species, and to regulate the marriages of its individual members. This is State socialism in its most extreme form, and is contrary to the spirit of a true liberalism, a true democracy, and a true Christianity.

The opposing position—the position of liberalism untainted by socialism—is that it is the duty of the State to see that as far as possible the social inequalities which arise through the individualistic organisation of society are removed or remedied, and that equality of opportunity is secured to each to make the best of his own individual life. In the educational sphere this implies that any obstacles in the way of a man's educating his children should be removed, if and in so far as these obstacles are irremovable by any private effort of his own, and that the opportunity of obtaining the best possible education should be open to the children of the poor if they are fitted by nature to profit by such an education. It further implies that the means of higher education, provided at the public expense, should not be wasted on the children of any class if by nature they are unfitted to benefit by the means placed at their disposal; *i.e.*, a national system of education must be democratic in the sense that the means of higher education shall be open to all, rich and poor, in order that each individual may be enabled to fit himself for the particular service for which by nature he is best suited. It must see, further, that any obstacles which prevent the full use of these means by particular individuals are, as far as may be possible, removed. A national system of education, on the other hand, must be aristocratic in the sense that it is selective of the best ability. Lastly, it must be restrictive, in order that the means of higher education may be utilised to the best advantage, and not misused on those who are unfitted to benefit therefrom.

Closely connected with the position that it is the duty of the State to see not merely to the adequate and efficient provision of the means of education, but also that the whole cost of the provision should be borne by the State, is the contention that because the State imposes a legal obligation upon the individual parent to provide a certain measure of education for his children, it is also a logical conclusion from this step that education should be free. "The object of public education is the protection of society, and society must pay for its protection, whether it takes the form of a policeman or a pedagogue."[13]

But the provision of the means of elementary education, and the imposing of a legal obligation upon each individual parent to utilise the means provided, is not merely or solely for the protection of society. Education confers not only a social benefit upon the community, but a particular benefit upon the individual. Its provision falls not within the merely negative benefits conferred by the State by its protection of the majority against the ignorance and wickedness of the minority, but it belongs to the positive benefits conferred by Government upon its individual members. The State in part undertakes the provision of the means of education, as Mill pointed out, in order to protect the majority against the evil consequences likely to result from the ignorance and want of education of the minority. As this provision confers a common benefit on all, so far, but only in so far, as education is protective, can its cost be laid upon the shoulders of the general taxpayer.

But the provision by the State of the means of education is not merely undertaken for the protection of any given society against the ignorance and the lawlessness of its own individual members, it is also undertaken in order to secure the increased efficiency of the nation as an economic and military unit in antagonism, more or less, with similar units. At the present day this is one main motive at work in the demand made for the better and more intensive training of the industrial classes. To secure the industrial and military efficiency of the nation is explicitly set forth as the main aim of the German organisation of the means of education. We may deplore this tendency of our times. We may condemn the rise of the intensely national spirit of the modern world, and regret that the ideal of universal peace and universal harmony between the nations of the earth seems to fade for ever and for ever as we move. But we have to look the facts in the face, and to realise that the educational system of a nation must endeavour to secure the industrial and military efficiency of its future members as a means of security and protection against other competing nations and as one of the essential conditions for the self-preservation of the particular State in that war of nation against nation which Hobbes so eloquently describes: "For the nature of war, consists not in actual fighting; but in the known disposition thereto, during all the time there is no assurance to the contrary." [14]

In so far, then, as the provision of education by the State is undertaken with this end in view, it may be maintained that part, at least, of the cost of its provision should be borne by the general taxpayer in return for the greater national and economic security which he enjoys through the greater efficiency of the nation as an economic and military unit.

But the spread and the higher efficiency of education confers in addition both a local and an individual benefit. It confers a local benefit, in so far as by its means advantages accrue to any particular district. It confers an individual benefit, in so far as through the means of education placed at his disposal the individual is enabled to attain to a higher degree of social efficiency than would otherwise have been possible.

Further, if we look at this question not from the point of view of benefit received, but from that of the obligation imposed, we reach a similar result. It is an obligation upon the State to see that the means of education and their due co-ordination and organisation are of such a nature both in extent and in quality as to furnish a complete system of means for the training up of the youth of the country to perform efficiently all the services required by such a complex community as the modern State. This duty devolves upon the State chiefly for the reason set forth by Adam Smith in his discussion of the functions of government. It is the duty of the sovereign, he declares, to erect and maintain certain "public institutions which it can never be for the interest of any individual to erect and maintain, because the profit could never repay the expense to the individual, or small number of individuals, though it may frequently do much more than repay it to a great society."[15]

It becomes further an obligation placed upon the local authority to aid the central authority of the State in the establishment and distribution of the means of education. The local authority by its more intimate knowledge of local circumstances is the most competent to judge of the nature of the education suited to serve its own particular needs, and is best qualified to undertake the distribution of the means.

But the obligation to take advantage of the means for the future benefit of his children is a moral obligation placed upon the shoulders of the individual parent. It becomes a legal obligation only when, and in so far as, the moral obligation is not realised by a certain number of the community. Certainly one reason for the making of the education of a man's children a legal obligation is the protection of society against the ignorance and wickedness of the minority, but the other and principal aim is to endeavour to secure that what at first was imposed as a merely external or legal obligation may pass into a moral and inherent obligation, so that the individual from being governed by outward restraint may in time be governed by an inward and self-imposed ideal.

It is no doubt difficult in any particular case to determine exactly what precise part of the cost should be allocated to each of the three benefiting parties, but in any national organisation of the means of education this threefold distribution of cost should somehow or other be undertaken.

From this it follows, that while it may legitimately be laid down that upon the State must fall the obligation of securing the adequate provision and the due distribution of the means of education, yet the further duty of the State in this respect is limited to the removing of obstacles which stand in the way of the fulfilment of the parent's obligation to educate his children, and to the securing to each child equality of opportunity to obtain an education in kind and quality which will serve to fit him hereafter to perform his special duty to society.

Although since 1891 elementary education has been practically free in this country and the whole cost of its provision is now undertaken at the public expense, yet except from the socialistic position that the provision of education is a communal and not a personal and moral obligation, this public provision of the funds for elementary education can be upheld from the individualistic point of view only on two grounds. In the first place, it might be maintained that the protective benefit derived from the imparting of the elements of education is so great to all that its cost may legitimately be laid upon the community in its corporate capacity. It is on this ground of education being beneficial to the whole society that Adam Smith declares that the expense of the institutions for education may, without injustice, be defrayed by the general contributions of the whole society. But at the same time Adam Smith recognises that education provides an immediate and personal benefit, and that the expense might with equal propriety be laid upon the shoulders of those benefited.

In the second place, it may be maintained that the imposition of school fees created such a hindrance in a large number of cases to the fulfilment of the moral obligation that it was expedient on the part of the State to remove this obstacle by freeing education as a whole. In support of this, it might be further urged that the difficulty of discriminating between the marginal cases in which the imposition of school fees really proved a hindrance and those in which it did not is great, and that the partial relief of payment of school fees laid the stigma of pauperism upon many who from unpreventable causes were unable to meet the direct cost of the education of their children.

But, except on the grounds that either the protective benefit to society is so great and so important, or that the charging of any part of the cost directly to the parent imposes a hindrance in a large number of cases, there is no justification for the contention that because the State compels the individual to educate his children, therefore the State should fully provide the means.

If this be so, then the further contention that the means of education from the elementary to the university stage should be provided at the public expense, and that no part of the cost should be laid directly upon the individual parent's shoulders, must also be judged to be erroneous.

The first duty of the State, in the matter of the provision of higher education, is limited to seeing that the provision of the means of higher education is adequate to the demand made for it; further, it may endeavour to encourage and to stimulate this demand in various ways. The means being provided, the second duty of the State is to endeavour to secure that any hindrance which might reasonably prevent the use of these means by those fitted to benefit therefrom should be removed. But the only justification for the interference of the State is that the compulsion exacted in the matter of taxes or otherwise is of small moment compared with the capacity for freedom and intellectual development set free in the individuals benefited. In other words, the cost involved by the removal of the hindrance must be reckoned as small compared with the ultimate good to the community as manifested in the higher development—in the higher welfare of its individual members.

But the practical realisation of the ideal need not involve that education should be free from the lowest to the topmost rung of the so-called educational ladder. It is indeed questionable whether the ladder simile has not been a potent instrument in giving a wrong direction to our ideals of the essential nature of what an educational organisation should aim at. Education should indeed provide a system of advancing means, but the system of means may lead to many and various aims instead of one. However that may be, what we wish to insist upon is that the State's duty in this matter can be fulfilled not by freeing education as a whole, but by establishing a system of bursaries or allowances, enabling each individual who otherwise would be hindered from using the means to take advantage of the higher education provided.

In the awarding of aid of this nature, the two tests of ability to profit from the education and of need of material means must both be employed. If the former test only is applied, then the result is that in many cases the advantage is secured by those best able to pay for higher education. If the objection be made that the granting of aid on mere need shown is to place the stigma of pauperism upon the recipient, then the only answer is that in so thinking the individual misconceives the real nature of the aid, fails to understand that it is help towards doing without help—aid to enable the individual to reach a higher and fuller development of his powers, both for his own future welfare and for the betterment of society.

FOOTNOTES:

[13] *National Education and National Life,* ibid. p. 101.

[14] Hobbes, *Leviathan,* p. 1. chap. xiii.

[15] Adam Smith, *Wealth of Nations,* ed. J. Shield Nicholson (Nelsons).

CHAPTER VI

THE RELATION OF THE STATE TO EDUCATION— MEDICAL EXAMINATION AND INSPECTION OF SCHOOL CHILDREN

In considering the question of the relation of the State to education, we have adopted the position that it is the duty of the State to see to the adequate provision of the means of education, to their due distribution and to their proper organisation. At the same time we found that the obligation of the State in this respect did not necessarily involve that the whole cost of this provision should be borne at the public expense, and that no part of the burden should be placed on the shoulders of the individual parents. As regards the provision of elementary education, we indeed found that the whole burden might be legitimately laid upon the general taxpayer, upon the grounds either that the protective benefit of elementary education to the community was great, or that the hindrance opposed by the imposition of school fees to the fulfilment of a man's moral obligation to provide for the education of his children was so general that a case might be made out for freeing elementary education as a whole. But except from the position that the provision of education was a communal and not a personal obligation, we found no grounds for the contention that education throughout its various stages should be a charge upon the community as a whole.

But the provision of the means of education may involve much more than the mere provision of adequately equipped school buildings and of fully trained teachers, and we have now to inquire what other provision is necessary in order to secure the after social efficiency of the children of the nation, and what part of this provision rightly may be included within the scope of the duties of the State.

Is the medical inspection of children attending Public Elementary Schools one of these duties, and, if so, what action on the part of the State does this involve?

The importance of the thorough and systematic medical examination of children attending school as a necessary measure to secure their after physical and economic efficiency as well as for their intellectual development and welfare during the school period has been recognised by many Continental countries. To take but one or two illustrative examples, we may note that in Brussels every place of public instruction is visited at least once in every ten weeks by one of the sixteen doctors appointed for this purpose. The school doctor amongst other duties has to report on the state of the various classrooms, their heating, lighting and ventilation, and also upon the condition in which he has found the playgrounds, lavatories and cloakrooms attached to the school. Cases of illness involving temporary absence from school are reported to him as well as the cases involving prolonged absence from school.

Children are medically examined upon admission to school, and a record is made of their age, height, weight, chest measurement, etc. "Any natural or accidental infirmity is chronicled, state of eyes and teeth, dental operations performed at school, etc. This examination is repeated annually, so as to keep a record of each child's physical development." Great attention, moreover, is paid to the cleanliness of the children attending school, and the children are examined daily by the teacher upon their entrance to school.[16]

In most of the large towns of Germany a system of periodical medical examination and inspection of children attending school has also been established. *E.g.*, in 1901 Berlin appointed ten doctors for this purpose, with the following amongst other duties:—

   1. To examine children on their first admission as to their fitness to attend school.

   2. To examine children with the co-operation of a specialist for the presence of defect in the particular sense organs (sight, hearing).

   3. To examine children who are supposed to be defective and who may require special treatment.

   4. To examine periodically the school buildings and arrangements and to report on any hygienic defects.[17]

In England, although there is no specific provision for the incurring of the expense of conducting the medical inspection of children attending the Public Elementary Schools, it is generally held that the expense may be legitimately included in the general powers assigned to educational authorities under the Act of 1870; and, especially since 1892, in several areas, a definite system of medical inspection has been established, and in many others there is a likelihood that some system of medical inspection will be organised in the immediate future. According to the Report of the Inter-Departmental Committee on the Medical Inspection and Feeding of School Children, published in November 1905, out of 328 local education authorities, 48 had established a more or less definitely organised system of medical examination, whilst in eighteen other districts teachers and sanitary officers had undertaken organised work for the amelioration of the physical condition of children attending Public Elementary Schools. As a rule, this inspection is limited "to the examination of the children and to the discovering of defects of eyesight, hearing, or physical development." When the existence of the defect is discovered, the parent is notified, but as a general rule the public authority does not include within its duties the treatment of the ailments and defects or the provision of remedial instruments when required.

Further, in no case has there been carried out a thorough anthropometric record, such as that in vogue in the schools of Brussels, of the condition of the physical nature of the child upon admission to school and his subsequent physical development.

In Scotland we find no general or adequate system of medical inspection carried out by the local school authorities. The Report of the Royal Commission on Physical Training (Scotland), issued in March 1903, declares, however, that such a system is urgently needed, mainly for remedial purposes. By this means defects in the organs of sight or hearing, in mental development, in physical weakness, or in state of nutrition, such as demand special treatment in connection with school work, might be detected, and by simple means removed or mitigated. But although in the Education (Scotland) Bill of 1905 provision was made for the institution of medical inspection at the public expense, yet through the failure of the Bill to pass nothing of a systematic nature has been done to organise the medical inspection of Elementary School children in any district in Scotland.

From this brief account of what either has been already done or is proposed to be done, it is apparent that there is a gradual awakening of the nation to the fact that the care of the physical nature of the child during the school period is of fundamental importance from the point of view of the future welfare and efficiency of the nation. In the endeavour to reach this aim it is necessary that the examination of the child should be undertaken in a systematic manner, and that means should be adopted for the remedy of any defects. In particular every child on admission to school should be examined in order to discover whether there is any defect present in the special organs of sense,[18] and periodical examinations should be made in order to discover whether the school work is tending to produce any injury to the various senses. For it is a well-known fact that often cases of seeming stupidity and seeming carelessness are not due either to the want of intelligence on the one hand or of inattention on the other, on the part of the child, but may be traced to slight defects of eyesight and of hearing. In order that they may discover these defects teachers ought to be trained in the observation of the main symptoms which imply defects, and should be practised in the art of applying the simpler and more obvious remedies for eye and ear defects. More difficult cases should be referred to the medical officer of the school. Again, it ought to be a matter of inquiry at the beginning of the school period as to whether the child possesses any physical defect which would make it difficult for him to undertake the full work of the school. In some cases it would be found that the child was altogether unable to undertake this work, and measures should be taken to remedy the defect before the child enters upon the school course. Lastly, it is now realised that more attention must be paid to the differences that exist between individual children, and that in the case of children with a low degree of intelligence it is much better both for themselves and for the school generally to institute special classes or special schools for their education.

But in order that this medical examination may be thoroughly and systematically carried out, special legislative authority must be given to education authorities to incur expense under this head, and regulations must be laid down by the central authority for the carrying out of this inspection so as to secure something like a uniform system of examination throughout the country. For this purpose there should be attached to each school area a medical officer, or officers, charged with the sole duty of attending to the hygienic conditions under which the school work is carried on, and of periodically examining the children attending the schools of his district.

That the duty of carrying out the medical examination of school children falls upon the State and should be met out of public funds may be justified on various grounds. In the first place, it is necessary as a measure of protection, in order to prevent the child's growing up imperfectly, and thus becoming in adult life a less efficient member of society. School work often accentuates certain troubles, and these if neglected tend gradually to render the individual more and more unfitted to undertake some special occupation in after-life. Any eye specialist could furnish evidence of numerous cases in which the eyes have been ruined through some slight defect becoming intensified through misuse.

In the second place, the examination for physical and mental defect cannot in a large number of cases be left to the self-interest and judgment of the individual parent, and unless undertaken by the public authority will not be undertaken at all.

In the third place, if it is left to merely voluntary agencies, it is imperfectly done, and in many cases recourse is had to the various voluntary agencies when the trouble has become acute, and in some cases impossible of remedy.

On these three grounds—of its necessity for the future public welfare, that the self-interest of the parent often proves but a feeble motive power, and that the voluntary agencies placed at the disposal of the poor are unable systematically to undertake this work—we may maintain that the duty may legitimately be laid upon the State.

But the further question as to how far it becomes the duty of the State to undertake the provision of remedial measures either in the way of supplying medical aid or in the provision in necessitous cases of remedial measures, as *e.g.* spectacles in the case of defective eyesight, is a question of much greater difficulty.

At present any positive help of this nature is the exception rather than the rule, and is undertaken by agencies worked on the voluntary principle, and the remedial measures adopted are limited to the treatment of certain minor ailments. *E.g.*, in Liverpool, Birmingham, and other places, Queen's nurses regularly visit the schools, and undertake either in school or at the homes of the children simple curative treatment of minor surgical cases. But while it may be held that the duty of the State is limited to the medical examination of school children in order to discover the presence of physical and mental defects, and that this being done, any further responsibility, whether in the way either of providing or procuring remedies, falls upon the individual parent, yet we have sufficient evidence to show that, in many cases, either through the poverty or the apathy and indifference of the parents, no steps are taken in the way of providing the necessary remedies, and as a consequence we have growing up in our midst children who in after-life will, through the lack of simple curative treatment undertaken at the proper time, become more or less socially inefficient.

Moreover, it is to be noted that in this matter the State has already recognised its public obligation to provide remedial aid in its provision for the education and lodging of the blind, the deaf and the dumb, and in the measures taken within recent years for the special education of the defective and the epileptic. The provision for these purposes may indeed be justified on the grounds that the expense of the education of children of the industrial classes so afflicted is beyond the powers of any one individual, or group of individuals, to supply, and that unless undertaken by the State it would not be efficiently made, with the consequence of throwing the maintenance hereafter of these particular classes upon the community: on the ground, therefore, of the future protective benefit to society, such expense may be legitimately laid upon the community as a whole. Further, in these cases, the danger of the weakening of the sense of parental responsibility is not an extreme danger to the Commonwealth, since the aid is definitely limited to a restricted number of cases, and since the moral obligation imposed upon the individual to provide for the education of his children could in many cases not be fulfilled without the by far greater portion of the expense being provided by means of public or voluntary aid.

In like manner, the expense of the special education of the morally defective in Industrial Schools and in other institutions may be justified on the ground of the present and future protective benefit to society. In these cases parental government has either altogether ceased or become too weak to act as an effective restraining force, and as a consequence the community for its own self-preservation has to undertake the control and education of the actual or incipient youthful criminal. In their Report the Royal Commissioners on Physical Training (Scotland) sadly declare that Industrial and similar institutions certainly give the boys and girls who come under their influence advantages in feeding and physical training which are not open to the children of independent and respectable though poor parents. *The contrast between the condition of children as seen in the poorer day schools and children in Industrial institutions, whose parents have altogether failed to do their duty, is both marked and painful.*[19]

And yet it might be urged that the protective benefit likely to be derived in the future by the provision of remedial means for the removal of the simpler defects in the case of the children of parents unable without great difficulty to supply these themselves is no less evident than in the more extreme cases. But here the only sound principle of guidance is to ask whether the remedial measures required are reasonably within the power of the parent to provide. If they are not, no community which exercises a wise forethought will suffer children to grow up gradually becoming more and more defective, more and more likely in after-life to be a burden upon its resources. But this question of the provision of remedial aid involves a much larger question, which we shall now discuss.

Appendix

As showing the need for the systematic examination of the special sense organs, I append a summary of the results arrived at and the conclusions reached by Dr. Wright Thomson after examination of the eyesight of children attending the Public Elementary Schools under the Glasgow School Board:—

> "The teachers tested the visual acuteness of 52,493 children, and found 18,565, or 35 per cent., to be below what is regarded as the normal standard.
>
> "I examined the 18,565 defectives by retinoscopy, and found that 11,209, or 21 per cent. of the whole, had ocular defects.

"The percentage with ocular defects was fairly constant in all the schools, but the percentage with defective vision was very variable—*i.e.*, many children with normal eyes were found to see badly.

"The proportion of these cases was highest in the poor and closely-built districts and in old schools, and was lowest in the better class schools and in those near the outskirts of the city.

"The proportion of such cases in the country schools of Chryston and Cumbernauld was much lower than in any of the city schools; and in Industrial Schools, where the children are fed at school, the proportion was lower than among Board School children of a corresponding social class.

"Defective vision, apart from ocular defect, seems to be due, partly to want of training of the eyes for distant objects, and partly to exhaustion of the eyes, which is easily induced when work is carried on in bad light, or the nutrition of the children defective from bad feeding and unhealthy surroundings.

"Regarding training of the eyes for distant objects, much might be done in the infant department by the total abolition of sewing, which is definitely hurtful to such young eyes, and the substitution of competitive games involving the recognition of small objects at a distance of 20 feet or more.

"Teachers can determine the visual acuteness, but they cannot decide whether or not an ocular defect is present.

"Visual acuteness, especially among poor children, is variable at different times.

"Teachers should have access to sight-testing materials at all times, and should have the opportunity of referring suspected cases for medical opinion.

"An annual testing by the teachers, followed by medical inspection of the children found defective, would soon cause all existing defects to be corrected, and would lead to the detection of those which develop during school life."

An examination of 502 children attending the Church of Scotland Training College School, Glasgow, as regards defects in eyesight and hearing, was made by Drs. Rowan and Fullerton respectively, with the following results:—

"As regards eyesight—

"61.55 per cent. were passed as normal, while of those defective 7.57 were aware of the fact; some few of these had already received treatment, but 30.88 were quite unaware that there was anything wrong, these unfortunates being expected to do the same work as, and hold their own with, their more fortunate classmates.

"As regards hearing—
    54.4 per cent. were found normal.
    27.6 "   " were defective.
    18.   "   " were distinctly defective."

I append the very valuable suggestions and conclusions of Dr. Rowan, who conducted the examination on the eyesight of children:—

"After examining 502 children, which involved the examination of 1004 eyes, one is forced to certain conclusions. These children are taken at random, and in this way they may be considered as a fair sample of their age and class.

"I think one of the first things that force themselves on our notice is the difficulties under which many of those children labour, and of which they, their parents and teachers are quite unaware. The children are considered dull, careless, or lazy, as the case may be: they themselves, poor unfortunates, do not know how to complain, and seem just to struggle along as best they can, though this struggle, without adequate result, must discourage them, and in this indirect way, too, make their future prospects more hopeless.

"Some would be considerably benefited by treatment and operation, or both, while for some little can be done. Some of those who could be benefited are deprived of help by their parents' ignorance or prejudice.

"In the case of those for whom little or nothing can be done, and whose sight is very defective, it seems to me the question ought to be raised as to whether their present mode of education should not be replaced by some other, which would endeavour to develop their abilities in other ways than through their eyesight; in short, they should have special training with the view of fitting them for some form of employment for which they are more fitted than the ordinary occupations of everyday life. This raises a difficult question, and each case would have to be settled on its merits. The difficulty must be faced; otherwise the children will simply drift and become idle and useless, while, if educated, at any rate partly, on the system for the blind, they would become useful members of society.

"I think no one, after studying the result of this examination of what may be by some considered a small number of children, can doubt that a thorough medical examination of all school children should be made when they enter school, and this examination repeated at regular intervals.

"I hold this applies not only to the children of the poor, but to children in all ranks of life, as one constantly, and that, too, in private practice, meets with cases where children are considered dull and lazy, while the real fault lies with the parents, who have not taken the trouble to ascertain the physical fitness or unfitness of their children.

"I am glad to say it is now becoming more common for children to be taken to the family doctor, to a specialist, or to both, to be thoroughly overhauled before starting school-life; and in many cases with most satisfactory results, as their training can be modified or treatment ordered which prevents the development of those pathological conditions which, in many cases, would limit the choice of occupation, or, if these are already present, they can at least be modified or even overcome.

"I wish to emphasise the fact that those thorough medical examinations should be repeated in the case of all children at regular intervals, as in this way alone can a proper physical standard be maintained, and deviations from the normal detected promptly and in many cases cured before the sufferer is aware of their presence.

"How often in examining our adult patients do we find them much surprised when they are told and convinced by actual proof that all their life they have depended on one eye only! This fact, of course, they sometimes accidentally discover for themselves, and come with the statement that the eye has suddenly gone blind. In the majority of these cases the weaker eye is useless, and the possibility of making it of any use is, at their age, practically *nil*."

FOOTNOTES:

[16] Cf. *Special Report on Educational Subjects,* vol. ii.

[17] Cf. *Report on Elementary Schools of Berlin and Charlottenburg,* by G. Andrew, Esq.

[18] Cf. Appendix, pp. 62-65.

[19] *Report Royal Commission on Physical Training* (*Scotland*), vol. i. (Neill & Co,. Edinburgh).

CHAPTER VII

THE RELATION OF THE STATE TO EDUCATION—THE FEEDING OF SCHOOL CHILDREN

A much more important and far-reaching question than that of the State provision for the medical examination and inspection of children attending Public Elementary Schools is the question of whether, and to what extent, the State should undertake the provision of school meals for underfed children.

Of the existence of the evil of under and improper feeding of children, especially in many of our large towns, there is no doubt. The numerous voluntary agencies which have been brought into existence to cope with the former are sufficient evidence that the evil exists and that it is of a widespread nature. Again, the high rate of infant mortality amongst the children of the lower classes is largely due to ignorance on the part of parents of the nature and proper preparation of food suitable for children. Further, the social conditions under which many of the poor live in our large towns is a contributing cause of this improper feeding. In many cases there is no adequate provision in the home for the cooking and preparation of food, and in others the absence of the mother at work during the day necessitates the children "fending" for themselves in the providing of their meals. However, in considering this question we must carefully distinguish between three distinct causes operating to produce the condition of underfeeding, and as a consequence resulting in three distinct classes of underfed children. As the causes or groups of causes are different in nature, so the remedies also vary in character. Moreover, in many cases we find all three causes operating, now one and now the other, to produce the chronic underfeeding of the child.

In the first place, the underfeeding of the child may arise through the temporary poverty of the parent due to his temporary illness or temporary unemployment. In normal circumstances, in these cases relief is best afforded by means of the voluntary agencies of society. In abnormal circumstances, such as are caused by a widespread depression of industry, the evil may be met by a special effort on the part of the voluntary agencies or by municipalities or other bodies providing temporary relief-work.

In the second place, the underfeeding of the child may be due to the chronic and permanent poverty of the parent. The wages of the breadwinner even when in full work may be insufficient to afford adequate support for a numerous family. This condition of things is not peculiar to Great Britain, but is a common characteristic in the life of the poor of all civilised nations. This is where the real sting of the problem of underfeeding lies, and the causes at work tending to produce this condition of things are too deep-seated and too widely spread to be removed by any one remedy. Moreover, in endeavouring to cure this disease of the Commonwealth we are ever in danger of perpetuating and intensifying the causes at work tending to produce the evil.

In the third place, the underfeeding of the child may arise through the indifference, the selfishness, or the vice of the parents. In such cases the parents could feed their children, but do not. Manifestly in cases of this character there is no obligation placed upon the State and no rightful claim upon any charitable agency to provide food for the children. To give aid simply weakens further the parental sense of responsibility, and leaves a wider margin to be spent on vicious pleasures. But while there is no obligation placed upon the State to provide the necessaries of life for the child, there is need and justification in such cases for the intervention of the State. There is need, for otherwise the child suffers through the criminal neglect of the parents, and the community must interfere for the sake of the future social efficiency of the individual and of the nation. There is justification, for here as in the case of the parents of the morally defective, parental responsibility has either ceased to act or become too weak a motive force to be effective in securing the welfare of the child. As the individual parent neglects his duty, so and to the corresponding degree to which this neglect extends, must the duty be enforced by the State. But in the enforcing of this or of any duty we must be quite sure that the neglect is really due to the weakened sense of responsibility of the parent, that it is a condition of things which he could remove if he had the moral will to do so, and that the neglect is not due to causes beyond the power of the parent to remove.

Cases in which there is culpable neglect of the child due not to poverty, but to the fact that the money which should go to the proper nutrition of the child is squandered in drink, or on other enervating pleasures, are therefore cases in which recourse must be had to measures which enforce upon the parent the obligation to feed and clothe his children. The really difficult question is as to the best means of enforcing this obligation. Manifestly to punish by fine or imprisonment does little in many cases to alleviate the sufferings of the children. The punishment falls upon them as well as upon the parent, and where the latter is dead to, or careless of, the public opinion of his fellows, it fails to initiate that reform of conduct which ought to be the aim of all punishment. If indeed by imposition of fine, or by imprisonment, the individual realises his neglect of duty, repents, and as a consequence reforms, then good and well, but as a rule the neglect of the child is in such cases a moral disease of long standing and not easily cured, and so we find often that neither punishment by fine nor imprisonment, even when repeated several times, is effective in making the parent realise his responsibility and reform his conduct. All the while the child goes on suffering. He is no better fed during the period of fine or imprisonment, and the wrath of the parent is often visited upon his unoffending head.

The second method of cure proposed is to feed the children at the public expense and to recover the cost by process of law. But the practical difficulties in carrying out this plan are similar in kind to those formerly experienced in the recovery of unpaid school fees. The cost of recovering is often greater than the expense involved, and as a consequence local authorities are not inclined to prosecute. Further, there is the difficulty of discriminating between underfeeding due to wilful and culpable neglect and underfeeding due to the actual chronic poverty of the parent. If this plan is to be effective, some simpler method of recovery of cost than that which now prevails must be adopted. *E.g.*, it might be enacted that the sum decreed for should be deducted from the weekly wages of the parent by his employer. Here again many difficulties would present themselves in the carrying out of this plan. In the case of certain employments this could not be done. In other cases, employers would be unwilling to undertake the invidious task. Moreover, the cost of collection might equal or be greater than the cost incurred. Above all, such a method would do little to alleviate the sufferings and better the nutrition of the child. In most cases the school provides but one meal a day. Experience has shown that in the case of children of the dissolute the free meal at the school means less food at home. Were the cost deducted from the weekly wages of the parent, the result would be intensified. So great have been the difficulties felt in this matter that with one or two exceptions no foreign country has made the attempt to recover the cost of feeding from the parent. Yet the disease requires a remedy. The evil is too dangerous to the future social welfare of the community to be allowed to go on unchecked and unremedied. Moreover, to endeavour to educate the persistently underfed children of our slums is to do them a twofold injury. By the exercises of the school we use up, in many cases, with little result, the small store of energy lodged in the brain and nervous system of the child, and leave nothing either for the repair of the nervous system or for the growth of his body generally. We prematurely exhaust his nervous system, and by so doing we hinder his bodily growth and development. To make matters worse, we often insist that the child in order to aid his physical development must undergo an exhausting system of physical exercises when what is most wanted for this purpose is good and nourishing food and a sufficiency of sleep. At the same time that we are neglecting the nutrition of his body we are spending an increasing yearly sum on the so-called education of his mind. What, then, is the remedy? If fining and imprisonment of the parent only accentuate the sufferings of the child, if they fail to make the parent realise his responsibility and reform his conduct, if the provision of a free meal at school means less food at home, then there is only one thorough-going remedy for the evil, and that is to take the child away from the parent, to educate and feed him at the public expense, and to recover the cost as far as possible from the parent. In Norway this drastic method has been adopted. Under a law passed on the 6th January 1896, the authorities are empowered "to place neglected children in suitable homes or families at the cost of the municipality, the parent, however, being liable, if called upon, to defray the cost."[20]

The reasons for taking this extreme step are obvious. By no method of punishing the persistently dissolute and neglectful parent can you be assured of securing the proper nutrition and welfare of the child. Parental affection in these cases is dead, and parental responsibility for the present and future welfare of the child has ceased to act as a motive force. As a consequence, the child grows up to be, at best, socially inefficient, and liable in later life to be a burden upon the community. In many cases, the evil and sordid influences of his home and social environment soon check any springs of good in his nature, and more than likely he becomes in later life not merely a socially inefficient member of the community but an active socially destructive agent. Hence, on the ground of the future protective benefit to society, on the ground of securing the future social efficiency of the individual, on the ground that it is only by some such system we can ever hope to raise the moral efficiency of the rising generation of the slums, the method above advocated is worthy of consideration.

Against the adoption of such a method of treatment of the dissolute parent many objections may be urged, and it would be foolish to minimise the dangers which might follow its systematic and thorough carrying into practice. But the possible injury to the community through the weakening of the sense of parental responsibility seems to me small in comparison with the future good likely to result from the increased physical, economic, and ethical efficiency of the next generation which might reasonably be expected to follow from the rigorous carrying out of such a plan for a time. The fear lest a larger and larger number of parents might endeavour to rid themselves of the direct care of their children, if this plan were adopted, need not deter us. If this plan were carried into practice, then some extension of the scope of the Industrial Acts would be rendered necessary, and some such extension seems to have been in the minds of the Select Committee in their Report on the Education (Provision of Meals) Bill, 1906, in considering their recommendations.[21]

But the importance of the two classes of cases already considered sinks into comparative insignificance compared with the third class of cases. Temporary underfeeding caused by temporary poverty can be met in many ways without to any appreciable degree lessening the sense of the moral obligation of the parent to provide the personal necessities of food and clothing for his children. In the case, again, of the persistently dissolute and neglectful parent, moral considerations have ceased to operate, and so the individual by some method or other must be forced to perform whatever part of the obligation can be exacted from him.

But in the third class of cases parental responsibility may be an active and willing force, yet the means available may be so limited in extent that the child is in the chronic condition of being underfed. No one who carefully considers the information recently supplied by the Board of Education as to the methods of feeding the children attending Public Elementary Schools in the great Continental cities and in America can arrive at any other conclusion than that here we are in the presence of an evil not local but general, and apparently incidental to the organisation of the modern industrial State. For whether by voluntary agencies, by municipal grants, or by State aid, every great Continental city has found it necessary to organise and institute some system of feeding school children.

The only inference to be drawn from such a condition of things is that in a large number of cases the normal wages of the labourer are insufficient to maintain himself and his family in anything like a decent standard of comfort. How large a proportion of the population of our great cities is in this condition it is difficult exactly to estimate, but there is no doubt that a very considerable number of cases of the chronic underfeeding of school children may be traced to the insufficiency of the home income to support the family. The moral obligation to provide the personal necessities of food and clothing for his children is active, but the means for the realisation of the obligation cannot be provided in many cases the endeavour fully to meet the needs of the child results in the lessened efficiency of the breadwinner of the family.

The real causes at work tending to keep the wages of the unskilled labourer ever hovering round a mere subsistence rate must be removed, if anything like a permanent cure of this social evil is to be effected. We must endeavour on the one hand to lessen the supply of unskilled labour. By so doing the reward of such labour will tend to be increased materially. On the other hand, we must during the next decade or two endeavour by every means in our power to ensure that a larger and larger number of the children of the very poor shall in the next generation pass into the ranks of skilled labour.

But in the meantime something must be done. The children are there; they still suffer; and their wrongs cry aloud for redress. It is certainly true that any aid given to the child will tend meanwhile to keep the wages at bare subsistence rates. It is also true that the distribution of relief only tends to make the poor comfortable in their poverty, instead of helping them to rise out of it. All this and much more might be urged against the demand to institute and organise the systematic public feeding of school children. But these evils are evils which fall upon the present adult population. Education has, however, to do with the future, with the next generation and not with this. Its aim is to secure that as large a number as possible of the children of the present generation will grow up to be economically and ethically efficient members of the community. To secure this end the problem of underfeeding is only one of the problems that must be solved. If we adopt some systematic plan for securing the full nutrition of the children of the present, this must go hand in hand with other remedies. During the stage of transition we shall have to take into account that for a time the wages of the poorest class of labourer will tend to remain at their present low rate; we shall have to face the danger that by giving such aid we may in some cases still further weaken the sense of moral obligation of the parents of the present generation. If, on the other hand, we do nothing, or if we look to the present voluntary agencies to go on doing what they can to remedy the evil, what then? Will the evil be lessened in the next generation? Assuredly not, if the experience of the present and of the past are safe guides as to what we may expect in the future.

Hence we have no hesitation in urging that the feeding of children attending the Public Elementary Schools should be organised on lines similar to the recommendations laid down in the *Special Report from the Special Committee on Education* (*Provision of Meals*) *Bill*, 1906.[22]

But if we carry out these recommendations and do nothing else, then it may be that we shall partially remedy the evil in the next generation, but we shall to a large extent perpetuate the present condition of things. Side by side with this, we must institute and set other agencies at work. By the institution of Free Kindergarten Schools in the poorer districts of our large towns, by postponing the beginning of the formal education of the child to a later age, by a scientific course of physical education, by better trade and technical schools, and if need be by the compulsory attendance of children at evening continuation schools, we must bend our every effort to secure that the ranks of the casual, the unskilled, and the unemployable shall be lessened, and the ranks of the skilled and intelligent worker increased.

As the freeing of elementary education can be justified on the ground that the education of the child is necessary for the future protection of the State, so on similar grounds it may be urged that the nutrition of the child is also necessary. Without this our merely educational agencies can never adequately secure the social efficiency of the coming generation. At the same time, unless in the future the need for free education and free food becomes less and less, and unless by the means sketched above we rear up a generation economically and morally independent, then truly we have not discovered the method by which man can be raised to independence and rationality.

Appendix

Recommendations of the Select Committee on Education (Provision of Meals) Bill, 1906.

"The evidence, verbal and documentary, placed before the Committee has led them to arrive at the following general conclusions:—

"1. That it is expedient that the Local Education Authority should be empowered to organise and direct the provision of a midday meal for children attending Public Elementary Schools, and that statutory powers should be given to Local Authorities to establish Committees to deal with school canteens.

"2. That such Committees should be composed of representatives of the Local Education Authority, representatives of the Voluntary Subscribers, and where thought desirable a representative of the Board of Guardians, and of the local branch of the Society for the Prevention of Cruelty to Children, where such exists. That the Head Teacher, the School Attendance Officer, and the Relieving Officer should work in association with such Committee.

"3. That power should be given for the Local Education Authorities, when they deem it desirable, to raise loans and spend money on the provision of suitable accommodation and officials, and for the preparation, cooking, and serving of meals to the children attending Public Elementary Schools.

"4. That only in extreme and exceptional cases, where it can be shown that neither the parents' resources nor Local Voluntary Funds are sufficient to cover the cost, and after the consent of the Board of Education as to the necessity for such expenditure has been obtained, a Local Authority may have recourse to the rates for the provision of the cost of the actual food; the local rate for this purpose to in no case exceed 1/2d. in the £.

"5. That the Local Education Authority should, as far as possible, associate with itself, and encourage the continuance of, voluntary agencies in connection with the work of feeding of children.

"6. That whatever steps may be necessary, by way of extension of the Industrial Schools and the Prevention of Cruelty to Children Acts or otherwise, should be taken to secure that parents able to do so and neglecting to make proper provision for the feeding of their children shall be proceeded against for the recovery of the cost; and that the Guardians, or where available the Society for the Prevention of Cruelty to Children, and not the Local Education Authority, be empowered to prosecute in any cases coming under the law in respect to the neglect of parents to make proper provision for the feeding of their children.

"7. That payment for meals, prior to the meal, whenever possible, should be insisted upon from the parents.

"8. That it is undesirable that meals should be served in rooms habitually used for teaching purposes, and that the Regulations of the Board of Education should carry this recommendation into effect.

"9. That whilst strong testimony has been placed before the Committee to the effect that the teachers have given and are giving admirable service in the way of supervising the provision of meals to the children, it is the opinion of the Committee that it ought not to be made part of the conditions attaching to the appointment of any teacher that he (or she) shall or shall not take part in dispensing meals provided for the children, and that the Board of Education should carry this recommendation into effect."

FOOTNOTES:

[20] Cf. Underfed Children in Continental and American Cities (presented to Parliament, April 1906).

[21] Cf. *Report on Education (Provision of Meals) Bill*, especially Recommendation 6, Appendix, p. 75.

[22] Cf. Appendix, p. 75.

CHAPTER VIII

THE ORGANISATION OF THE MEANS OF EDUCATION

Throughout we have assumed that it is the duty of the State to see to the adequate provision, to the due distribution, and to the proper co-ordination of all the agencies of education, and we have taken up this position mainly on the ground that neither the adequate provision nor the proper co-ordination of the means of education can be safely left to the self-interest of the individual or any group of individuals. If left to be accomplished by purely voluntary agencies, both the provision and the co-ordination will remain imperfect, and as a nation we can no longer neglect the systematic organisation and grading of the means of education.

But a misapprehension must first be removed. In declaring that all the agencies of formal education should be under control of the State, it is not to be inferred that this control should be bureaucratic. In many minds State control is synonymous with government by inspectors and other officials of the central authority. But bureaucratic control in a nation whose government is founded on a representative basis is a disease rather than a normal condition of such government. In a country where the sovereign power is vested in an individual or in a limited number of individuals, bureaucratic control is and must be an essential feature of its government. On the other hand, where the government is founded upon the representative principle, the appearance of bureaucracy is an indication of some imperfection in the organisation of the State itself. The introduction of the representative principle may have been too premature or its extension too rapid, and as a consequence the government of the people by themselves is ineffective through the general want of an enlightened self-interest amongst the majority of the nation. In such a condition of affairs, if progress is to be made, it can only be accomplished effectively through an enlightened minority forcing its will upon the unenlightened and ignorant majority, and as a result we may have the creation of an army of official inspectors whose chief duty becomes to secure that the will of the central authority is realised. In such a condition of things the tendency ever is for more and more power to fall into the hands of the permanent officials.

But this condition of things may arise in a government founded upon the representative principle in another way. The organs through which the will of the people makes itself known may be imperfect, so that as a consequence it fails to find adequate expression, or its expression is felt only at infrequent intervals. If, for example, the central authority is so overburdened with work that little or insufficient attention is given to many matters of supreme importance for the welfare of the nation, then it follows that more and more power will pass into the hands of its executive and advisory officers. This condition of things will be further intensified if the governing bodies charged with the local control of national affairs are too weak or too unenlightened to make their voice effective. Now, the tendency to the bureaucratic control of the educational affairs of our own country may be traced to all three causes. The want of an enlightened self-interest in the matter of education amongst a large number of the people, the ineffectiveness of Parliament to deal thoroughly with purely educational questions, and the weakness in many cases of the local governing bodies have all contributed to the gradual creation of the bureaucratic control of education in Great Britain. But this form of control is not entirely evil, and in certain cases it may be a necessary stage in the development of a democracy passing from unenlightenment to enlightenment. The remedies for this imperfection, this disease of representative government in the matter of educational control, are (1) the spread of a more enlightened self-interest as to the value of education as a means of securing the social efficiency of the nation and of the individual, (2) the effective control of education by the central authority, and (3) the strengthening of the local authorities by devolving upon them more and more important educational duties. By this means the control of education by the State will become more and more the control of the people by themselves and for themselves, and the chief function of officials and inspectors will then be to advise central and local authorities how best to realise the educational aims desired by the common will of the people.

Let us now consider the main principles which should guide the State in her organisation of the means of education.

In the first place, and upon this all are agreed, the control of all grades of education, primary, secondary, and technical, should be entrusted to one body in each area or district. For there can be no co-ordination established between the work of the various school agencies, and there can be no differentiation of the functions to be undertaken by the various types of school, until there has been established unity of control.

In England, by the Act of 1902, a great step was taken towards the unification of all the agencies of education. According to its provisions, the School Board system was abolished. "Every County Council and County Borough Council, and the Borough Councils of every non-county borough with a population of over 10,000, and the District Council of every urban district with a population over 20,000, became the local education authority for elementary education, while the County Council and the County Borough Council became the authorities for higher education, *with the supplementary aid of the Councils of all non-county boroughs and urban districts*." By this means the unification of educational control has been realised, and already in many districts of England much has been done to further the means of higher education and to co-ordinate this stage with the preceding primary stage.

In Scotland the question of the extension of the area of educational control and of the unification of the various agencies directing education still awaits solution. Several plans have been put forward to effect these ends.[23]

In the first place, it has been proposed to retain the present parish School Boards for the purpose of elementary education, and to combine two or more School Boards for the purposes of providing secondary and technical education. This plan, however, meets with little favour. It would be difficult to carry into practice, and if realised would imperfectly fulfil the end of co-ordinating the work of the various school agencies. Its only recommendations are its apparent simplicity, and the fact that it could be carried out with the least possible change in the existing conditions.

In the second place, it is proposed to retain the School Board system, but to extend the area over which any particular educational authority exerts its control, and to place under its direction all grades of education. In the practical carrying out of this plan the present district areas of counties selected for other purposes have been proposed as educational units. On the other hand, it has been declared that in many cases these areas are unsuitable for educational purposes, and it has been proposed that new areas should be delimited for this purpose.

The chief merit, if it be a merit, of this plan is the retention in educational control of the *ad hoc* principle—*i.e.*, of the principle of entrusting one single national interest to a body charged with the sole duty of conserving and furthering the interest. The only reasons advanced are the great importance of the educational interest and the fear that if it is entrusted to bodies charged with other duties this interest may tend to be neglected. But although both sentiment and the interests of political parties are involved in the advocacy of the *ad hoc* principle, it must be kept in mind that the School Board system in Scotland is universal and that the difficulties of the system which prevailed in England before its abolition do not exist in Scotland. As a consequence, it has been much more effective in Scotland than in England, and has a much firmer hold on the sentiments of the people.

In the third place, it has been proposed to hand over the educational duties of the country to the County Councils and to the Burgh Councils of the more important towns, to adopt, in principle, a system of educational control similar to that established in England by the Act of 1902.

Many reasons may be urged for the adoption of the last-named plan, and we shall briefly state the more important.

1. An *ad hoc* authority by its very nature is necessarily weaker than an authority entrusted not merely with the care of a single interest but with the care of the public interests as a whole. If there is to be decentralisation of any part of the functions of the central authority, then any form of decentralisation which consists in the handing over of particular interests to different local bodies, however it may be for the advantage of the particular interest is radically bad for the general interests of the community. The calling into existence of a number of local authorities each having the care of one particular interest, each pursuing its own aim independently and without consideration of the differing and often conflicting aims of the other bodies, each having the power of rating for its own particular purpose

without any regard for the general interest of the taxpayer, is radically an unsound form of decentralisation.

2. The establishment of such a form of control fails, and must necessarily fail, in the local authorities securing the maximum of freedom and the minimum of interference from the executive officers of the central legislative authority. So long as the separate interests of the community are entrusted to different local authorities, so long must there remain to the central authority and to its executive officers the power of regulating and harmonising the various and often contending interests so as to secure that the general interest of the individual does not suffer, and the more keenly each particular body furthers the particular interest entrusted to its care the greater is the necessity for this central control and interference, and that the central control should be effective.

3. The separation of the so-called educational interests from the other interests of the community is not for the good of education itself. The real educational interests which have to be determined by the adult portion of the community are the exact nature of the services which a nation such as ours requires of its future members. This determined, the method of their attainment is best entrusted to the educational expert. The first-named end will be better realised by a body composed of men of diverse interests than by one which is made up of men with one intense but often narrow interest.

4. The larger the powers entrusted to any body and the more freedom possessed by it in devising and working out its schemes, the better chance there is of attracting the best men in the community to undertake the work.

5. It is questionable whether the interests of the teacher would not be better furthered by a local authority entrusted with the care of the interests of the community as a whole than by a body having charge of education alone. Men entrusted with the larger interests of the community are usually more ready to take wider views than the man who is narrowed down to one interest. As a rule, they know the value of good work done, and are ready and willing to pay for it wherever they find it.

6. Lastly, we may urge the test of practical experience. In England, and especially in London, since the control of education has passed into the

hands of the County Councils a great advance has been made both in the furthering and in the co-ordination of the means of education.

Whether ultimately the control of education be vested in District School Boards or in the County and Burgh Councils, one reform is urgently needed in Scotland, and this is the extension of the area of educational control, under a strong local authority, and with the entire control of elementary, secondary, and technical education.

In the second place, whatever the area of control chosen it should be of such a nature as to admit within its bounds of schools of different grades and of different types, so that children may pass not only from the Elementary School to the Secondary, but may pass to the particular type of Secondary or Higher School which is best fitted to prepare them for their future life's work. In many cases, in Scotland, we cannot make the same clear distinction between the various types of school as they do in Germany, but must remain content with the division of a school into departments; yet in our large towns and in our most populous centres of industry we must establish schools of different types and with differing particular ends in view.

The third principle of organisation follows from the second. We must see that our educational system is so organised as to provide an efficient and sufficient supply of all the services which the community requires of its individual members. In particular, our Higher School system must be designed not merely for the supply of the so-called learned professions, but must also make due and adequate provision for the training of those who in after-life are destined for the higher industrial and commercial posts. In particular, we must see that there is due provision of Trade and Technical Schools, where our future artisans may become acquainted with the theoretical principles underlying their particular art.

Fourthly, we must endeavour to make our Elementary School system the basis and point of departure of all further and higher education. This would not involve that every child should be educated at a Primary and State-aided School, but it does mean and would involve that the Preparatory departments of our present Secondary Schools should model their curriculum on the lines laid down in our Elementary Schools.

Fifthly, in the organisation of the means of education, our system, as we have already pointed out, must be democratic in the sense that the means of higher education shall be open to all, rich and poor, in order that each may be enabled to find and thereafter to fit himself for that particular employment for which by nature he is best suited. It must further be aristocratic in the sense that it is selective of the best ability; and finally, it must be restrictive in order that the means of higher education may be utilised to the best advantage, and not misused on those who are unfitted to benefit therefrom.

Unity of control; adequacy of area; schools of various types, sufficient in number, and suited to meet the need for the supply of the various services required by the State; a common basis in elementary education; means of higher education open to all who can profit thereby; selection of the best; restriction of those unable to benefit from higher education—these are the principles which must in the future guide the State organisation of the means of education.

FOOTNOTE:

[23] For a fuller discussion of this question, see *Scotch Education Reform*, by Dr. Douglas and Professor Jones (Maclehose).

CHAPTER IX

THE AIM OF PHYSICAL EDUCATION

"A sound mind in a sound body is a short but full description of a happy state in this world. He that has these two has little more to wish for, and he that wants either of them will be but little the better for anything else."[24] In these words Locke sets forth for all time what should be aimed at in the physical education of the child, and in the light of modern physiological psychology the position must be emphasised anew that one of the essential conditions of sound intellectual and moral vigour is sound physical health, and that body and mind are not things apart, but that the health of the one ever conditions and is conditioned by the health of the other.

Moreover, at the present time, it is all the more necessary to insist upon the need for the systematic care of the physical culture of the child, since in many cases the conditions under which the children of the poor live in our great towns are most prejudicial to the full and free development of the organs of the body. The narrow, overbuilt streets in the poorer parts of our towns, the overcrowding of the people in tenements, the unhygienic conditions under which the vast majority of our very poor live and sleep, are all active forces in preventing the full and free development of the physical powers of the child. Thus the purely educational problem of how best to promote the physical health and development of the child by the systematic exercises of the school is involved in the much larger and more important social problem of how to better the conditions under which the very poor live. The agencies of the school can do little permanently to improve the physique of the children until, concurrently with the school, society endeavours to improve the social conditions under which the poorest of the population of our great cities herd together. For a similar reason much of the endeavour of the school to found and establish in the child's mind interests of social worth is counteracted by the evil influence of its home and social environment. If the physical, economic, and ethical efficiency of the children of the slums is ever to be secured, if we are ever to attain a permanent result, then concurrently with the creation of new and higher social interests must go hand in hand changes in the social environment of the child. Mere betterment of the physical conditions under which our slum population live is of no avail unless at the same time we have a corresponding change in the slum mind by the rise and prevalence of a higher ideal of the physical and material conditions under which their lives ought to be spent.

For experience has shown in many cases that the mere betterment of the material conditions under which the poor live without any corresponding change of ideals soon results in the re-creation of the miserable conditions which formerly prevailed. On the other hand, the mere instilling of new ideals into the minds of the rising generation will effect little, if during the greater part of the school period and altogether afterwards we leave the child to overcome the evil influences of his environment as best he may. The ideals of the school are too weak, too feebly established, to prevail against the ever present and ever potent influences of the environment unless side by side with the rise of the new ideals we at the same time endeavour to lessen, if we cannot altogether remove, the obstacles which prevent their realisation and prevalence. This problem of how to raise by education and by means of the other social agencies at work the children of the slums to a higher ideal of life and conduct and to secure their future social efficiency is the most urgent problem of our day and generation. Mere school reforms in physical and intellectual education will effect little unless the other aspects of the problem are attacked at the same time.

Further, our school system, which requires that the child should restrain his instinctive tendencies to action, and for certain hours each day assume a more or less passive and cramped attitude, is also prejudicial to the development and free play of the organs of the body which have entrusted to them the discharge of certain functional activities.

Hence the evil effects of the school itself must be removed or remedied by some means having as their aim the increased functional activity of the respiratory and circulatory systems of the body. And therefore the aim of any system of physical exercises should be not merely increase of bone and development of muscle but also the sustaining and improving of the bodily health of the child by "expanding the lungs, quickening the circulation, and shaking the viscera." This, as we shall see later, is not the only aim of physical education. It may further aid in mental growth and development, and be instrumental in the production of certain mental and moral qualities of value both to the individual and to the community.

Another cause operating in the school to prevent the full and free development of the body is the method of much of the teaching which prevails. A quite unnecessary strain is often put upon the nervous system of the child, and as a consequence a lassitude of body results which physical exercise not only does not tend to remove but actually tends to increase. Methods of teaching which fail to arouse any inherent interest in the attainment of an end of felt value to the child require for the evoking and maintaining of his active attention the operation of some powerful indirect interest, and if persisted in, such methods soon result in the overworking and exhaustion of some one particular system of nervous centres, and in the depletion through non-nutrition of other centres. As a consequence, the child is unable to take any part in physical exercises or in school games with profit to himself. He is content to loaf and do as little as he can. The evil is further intensified if there is also present under or improper nutrition of the child.

Thus along with our schemes for the physical education of the child we must endeavour to improve the methods of our teachers, to make them understand that experiences acquired through the arousing of the direct interest of the child are acquired at the least physiological cost, and to make them realise under what conditions this direct interest can be aroused and maintained. No one indeed wishes to make everything in the school pleasant to the child, or to reduce self-effort to a minimum. But effort and interest are not opposed terms. The effort which is evoked in the realisation of an interest or end of felt value is the only kind of effort which possesses any educational value. The effort which is called forth in the finding and establishing of a system of means towards an end which the child fails to see, and which, as a consequence, rouses no direct interest in its attainment, is an effort which should for ever be banished from the schoolroom. Such, *e.g.*, is the effort evoked in the mere cramming of empty lists of words or dates or facts. Little mental good results from such a process, and the physiological cost is often great.

Let us now consider the conditions necessary for sound physical health, and inquire how far the school agencies can aid in the providing of these conditions: they are mainly four in number. In the first place, in order to secure the full growth and development of the bodily powers, there is needed a sufficiency of food. But mere sufficiency is not enough, the food must be varied in quality in order to meet the various needs of the body, and must be prepared in such a way as to be readily assimilated and rendered fit for the nutrition of both body and mind. Manifestly the home ought to be the chief agent in providing for this need. But, as we have seen in considering the problem of the feeding of school children, the home in many cases is unable adequately to provide for it, and, for a time at least, some method of public provision of good and wholesome food for the children of the poor may be rendered necessary. But much of the physical evil results from improper nutrition; and here the school agencies may do a great deal in the future by furthering the teaching of domestic science to the girls of the working classes. Such teaching, however, if it is to be effective, must be real and must take into account the actual conditions under which their future lives are to be spent. At the present time much of the teaching is valueless, through its neglect of the actual income and resources of the working man's home.

The second condition necessary for bodily growth and development is a sufficiency of pure air. This is necessary, since the oxygen of the air is not only the active agent in the maintenance of life, but is also requisite for the combustion of the foodstuffs conveyed into the body. Much has been done within recent years in our schools to provide well-ventilated classrooms and to instruct teachers how to keep the air of the school pure. Here again the problem is to a large extent a social one, involving the better housing of our great town population.

A third condition necessary for the physical development of the child is sleep sufficient in quantity and good in quality. The weak, puny children in arms to be seen in our crowded slums owe their condition, in many cases, to the want of sound sleep, to the fact that they never are allowed to rest, as much as to the under and improper feeding to which they are subjected. As we shall see in the next chapter, much might be done by the establishment of Free Kindergarten Schools in our overcrowded districts to alleviate the lot and to better the education of the very young children of the poor.

But in addition to the three conditions already named, which may be classed together as the nutritive factors in bodily growth, there is a fourth condition essential for all development, whether bodily or mental—viz., exercise. For "development is produced by exercise of function, use of faculty.... If we wish to develop the hand, we must exercise the hand. If we wish to develop the body, we must exercise the body. If we wish to develop the mind, we must exercise the mind. If we wish to develop the whole human being, we must exercise the whole human being."[25]

But any form of exercise will not do. The exercise which is given must be given at the right time, must be in harmony with the nature of the organ exercised, and must be proportioned to the strength of the organ, if true development is to be attained.

In order to understand this in so far as it bears upon the aims which we should set before us in the physical education of the child, it is necessary that we should understand what modern physiological psychology has to teach us of the nature of the nervous system.

If the reader will look back to an earlier chapter,[26] he will find that education was defined as the process by which experiences are acquired and organised in order that they may render the performance of future action more efficient, or alternatively it is the process by which systems of means are formed, organised, and established for the attainment of various ends of felt value. The establishment of these systems of means is only possible because in the human infant the nervous system is relatively unformed at birth, is relatively plastic, and so is capable of being organised in such and such a definite manner. On the other hand, in many animals the nervous system of each is definitely formed at birth; it is so organised that experience does little to add to or aid in its further development. Now, while the nervous system of the child at birth is not so definitely organised as that of many animals, yet on the other hand it is not wholly plastic, wholly unformed, so that, as many psychologists and educationalists once believed, it can be moulded into any shape we please.

Rather, we have to conceive of the nervous system of the human infant as made up of a series of systems at different degrees of development and with varying degrees of organisation.[27] Some centres, as *e.g.* those which have to do with the regulation of certain reflex and automatic actions, start at once into full functional activity; others, as *e.g.* those which have to do with purely intellectual functions, are relatively unformed and unorganised at birth, and become organised as the result of conscious effort, as the result of an educational process, as the result of acquiring, organising, and establishing experiences for the attainment of ends of acquired value.

Between the systems at the lowest level and those at the highest we have centres of varying degrees of organisation at birth. Moreover, these centres of the middle level reach their full maturity at different rates. The centres, *e.g.*, which have to do with the co-ordination of hand and eye and with the attainment of control over the limbs of the body reach their full functional activity before, *e.g.*, the centres having control of the lips and speech. The centres, again, which have to do with the co-ordination of the sensory material derived through the particular senses are still longer in reaching their full functional activity, while the higher intellectual centres may not reach their highest power until well on in life. Hence, since education is the process of acquiring experiences that shall modify future activity, it can do little positively to aid the development of the lowest centres; it can do more to modify the development of the middle centres; while the highest centres of all are in great part organised as the result of direct individual experience.

As regards the systems of the lowest level, what we have then to aim at is to allow them free room for growth, and to correct as far as possible faults due either to the imperfections of nature or to the unnatural conditions under which the child lives. So long as these systems are provided with nutrition and allowed freedom in performing their functions, we are unaware of their existence. We, *e.g.*, only become aware that we possess a circulatory system or a respiratory or a digestive system when the functional activity of these organs is impeded. The opinion, therefore, that physical exercise has for its chief aim the sustaining and improving of the bodily health is no doubt true and correct, but it is not the only aim. On this view we are considering only the lowest system of centres, and devising means by which we may maintain and improve their functional activity. Moreover, it is necessary to endeavour to secure the free development of these centres and their unimpeded functional activity, because otherwise the development of the higher centres is hindered, and the whole nervous system rendered unstable and insecure.

But a wise system of physical education must take into account the fact that a carefully selected and organised system of exercises can do much for the development of the centres of the middle level which have to do with the proper co-ordination of various bodily movements. These are only partly organised at birth, and education—the acquiring and organising of experiences—is necessary for their due organisation and their adaptation as systems of means for the attainment of definite ends. It is for this reason that the beginning of the formal education of the child at too early an age is physiologically and psychologically erroneous. In doing this we are neglecting the lower centres at the time when by nature they are reaching their full functional activity, and exercising the higher which are at an unripe stage of development. Moreover, lower centres not exercised during the period when they are attaining their full development never attain the same functional development if exercised later. Hence the difficulty of acquiring a manual dexterity later in life. Again, it is on this theory of lower and higher centres maturing at different rates and attaining their full functional activity at different times that we now base our education of the mentally defective. We must organise the lower centres; we must educate the mentally defective child to get control over these already partially organised centres, before we begin to educate the higher and less organised centres. Moreover, it is only in so far as we can secure this end that we can stably build up and organise the higher centres of the nervous system. Hence also such qualities as alertness in receiving orders and promptness and accuracy in carrying them out are, at first, best learned through the organising and training of the centres of the middle level. What we really endeavour to do here is to organise and establish systems of means for the attainment of definite ends, which through their systematic organisation can be brought into action when required promptly and quickly, and once aroused work themselves out with a minimum of effort and with a low degree of attention, so that their performance involves the least possible physiological cost.

From this the reader will understand that the aim of physical education is the aim of all education, viz., to acquire and organise experiences that will render future action more efficient.

Moreover, the early training of the centres of the middle level is important for the after technical training of our workmen. The boy or girl who has never been educated in early life to co-ordinate and carry out bodily movements promptly and accurately is not likely to succeed in after-life in any employment which requires the ready and exact co-ordination of many movements for the attainment of a definite end. The proper physical education of the child is therefore necessary for the securing of the after economic efficiency of the individual, and it can also by the development of certain mental and moral qualities be made instrumental in the development of the ethically efficient person.

We must now briefly note two other educational agencies which may be employed in the securing of the physical and mental efficiency of the child—play and games. Psychologically, games stand midway between play and work. In play we have an inherited system of means evoked into activity and carried out to an end for the pure pleasure derived from the activity itself. Such systems at first are imperfectly organised, but through the experience derived the systems become more and better adapted for the attainment of the ends which they are intended to realise. In games, on the other hand, the activity is undertaken for an end only partially connected with the means by which it is attained, whilst in work the means may have no intrinsic connection with the end desired. Hence the effort of a disagreeable nature which work often evokes.

In animals fully equipped at birth by means of instinct for the performance of actions the play-activity is altogether absent. Their lives are wholly business-like. On the other hand, in the higher animals, whose young have a period of infancy, play is nature's instrument of education. By means of it the systems of the middle level which form the larger part of the brain equipment of the higher animals are gradually organised and fitted for the attainment of the ends which in mature life they are intended to realise. Play is their education—is the means by which nature works in order that experiences may be acquired and organised that shall render future action more efficient. Without this power, "the higher animals could not reach their full development; the stimulus necessary for the growth of their bodies and minds would be lacking."[28]

Play also is nature's instrument in the education of the young child. The first and most important part of his education is obtained by this means, and, on the basis thus laid, must all after-education be built. Hence the importance in early life of allowing full freedom for the manifestation of this activity. Hence also the very great importance of securing that the children of the poor should be provided with the means of realising the playful activities of their nature and of being stimulated and encouraged to play. Hence one aim of the Kindergarten School is to utilise the play-activity of the child in the development of his body and mind.[29]

The third agency which we may employ in developing the physical powers of the child is that of games. Games, however, are not merely useful as means for the attainment of the physical development of the boy or girl; they also may be made instrumental in the creation and fostering of certain mental and moral qualities of the greatest after-value to the community. No one acquainted with the important part which games perform in the life of the Public School boy can doubt their great educational value. By means of them the boy acquires experiences which in after-life tend to make more efficient certain classes of actions essential for any corporate or communal life. In the playing-fields he learns what it is to be a member of a corporate body whose good and not the attainment of his own private ends must be the first consideration. Through the medium of the games of the school he may get to know the meaning of self-sacrifice, of working with his fellows for a common end or purpose, and of sinking his own individuality for the sake of his side. In addition he learns the habits of ready obedience to superior knowledge and ability; to submit to discipline; and to undergo fatigue for the common good. If found worthy, he may learn how to command as well as to obey, to think out means for the attainment of ends, and to know and feel that the good name of the school rests upon his shoulders. These and other qualities similar in character may be created and established by means of the games of the school. And just as the utilising of the play-instinct is nature's method of education in the fitting of the young animal and the young child to adapt itself in the future to its physical environment, so we may lay down that the games of the school may be largely utilised as society's method of fitting the individual to his after social environment, and in training him to understand the true meaning and the real purport of corporate life.

On account, however, of the vast size of many of our Public Elementary Schools and for other reasons, such as the limited playground accommodation in many cases and the want of playing-fields, organised games play but a small part in the physical and moral education of the children attending such schools. But even here much more might be done than is done at present by the teachers in the playground to encourage the simpler playground games, and "to replace the disorganised rough and tumble exercises which characterise the activities of so many of our poorer population by some form of organised activity."[30] The aimless parading of our streets by the sons and daughters of the working and lower middle classes in their leisure time, the rough horseplay of the youth of the lowest classes, are due in large measure to the fact that during the school period they have not been habituated to take part with their fellows in any form of organised activity, have never realised what a corporate life means, and as a consequence are devoid of any social interests.

One other question must be briefly considered, viz., How far should we in the physical education of the youth keep in view the end of securing the military efficiency of the nation? As Adam Smith pointed out, the defence of any society against the violence and invasion of other independent societies is the first duty of the sovereign. "An industrious, and upon that account a wealthy nation is of all nations the most likely to be attacked, and unless the State takes some measures for the public defence, the natural habits of the people render them altogether incapable of defending themselves."[31] He further asserts that "even though the martial spirit of the people were of no use towards the defence of the society, yet to prevent that sort of mental mutilation, deformity, and wretchedness which cowardice necessarily involves in it, from spreading themselves through the great body of the people, it would still deserve the most serious attention of Government."[32]

On these three grounds, then, that the defence of the country is the first duty of every Government and therefore the first duty of every citizen, that a nation engaged in commerce tends to render itself unfit to defend itself unless means are devised to keep alive the patriotic spirit, and that the keeping alive of the patriotic spirit is useful for the cultivation of certain necessary social qualities, we may maintain that the military efficiency of the youth should be included amongst the aims of any national system of physical education. If the emphasis which is laid upon the securing of the after military efficiency of the youth of the nation occupies too prominent a place in the schemes of physical education of some Continental countries, we on the other hand have almost wholly neglected this aspect of the question. Every encouragement therefore should be given to the formation of cadet and rifle corps in the Secondary Schools of the country and in the Evening Continuation Schools attended by the sons of the working classes. The time when systematic instruction in military exercises and in the use of arms shall form part of every youth's education has not yet arrived, but the necessity for some such step looms already on the horizon.

FOOTNOTES:

[24] Locke's *Thoughts on Education*.

[25] Bowen's Froebel (Great Educator Series), p. 48.

[26] Cf. chap. ii.

[27] Cf. MacDougall's *Physiological Psychology* (Dent); *also* Sir James Crichton Browne's article on "Education and the Nervous System," in Cassell's *Book of Health*.

[28] *Principles of Heredity*, ibid. p. 242.

[29] Cf. next chapter.

[30] *Suggestions for the Consideration of Teachers* (English Board of Education), chapter on Physical Education.

[31] Adam Smith, *Wealth of Nations*, p. 292.

[32] *Ibid.* p. 329.

CHAPTER X

THE AIM OF THE INFANT SCHOOL

It is needless to point out that the method of educating the infant mind is the method of all education—viz., the regulation of the process by which experiences are acquired and organised so as to render the performance of future action more efficient. This, as we shall see later, is the fundamental truth at the foundation of the Kindergarten method of Froebel, and it must guide and control our conduct not only during the earlier stages but throughout the whole process of education.

Moreover, since the early acquisitions of the child are the bases upon which all further knowledge and practice are founded, we must realise how important these first experiences are for the whole future development of the child. Further, we have seen that all education—all acquiring and organising of experience in early life—must be motived by the felt desire to satisfy some instinctive need of the child's nature, and that it is these instinctive needs which determine the nature and scope of his early activities.

Later, indeed, acquired interests may be grafted upon the innate and instinctive needs, but at the beginning and during his first years the child's whole life is determined by the primitive desires of human nature.

Now, the first instinctive need which requires the aid of education is the need felt by the child to acquire some measure of control over his bodily movements and over the things in his immediate physical environment. Hence the first stage in education is the regulation of the process by which the child acquires and organises those experiences which shall give him this control. Nature herself indeed provides the means for the attainment of this end, but education can do much to aid in the attainment and to shorten the period of incomplete attainment. By means of the assistance given, the control exercised and the direction afforded, we enable the child to organise the lower centres of the nervous system which have to do with the control of the larger bodily movements, and thus establish organised systems of means for the attainment of certain definite ends.

The second stage supervenes when the need is felt by the child for some measure of control over his social environment. For the young child soon realises that it is only in so far as he can exert some influence over the persons intimately connected with his welfare that he can make his wants known and find means for the satisfaction of his desires. Hence arises the need for some method of communication with his fellows, and from this springs the desire for some system of signs and for a language to enable him to make his wants known. Chiefly by means of the educative process of imitating the experiences of others, he gradually acquires a language and finds himself at home in his social world.

During this period the centres called into activity, developed, and organised are mainly those connected with the lip and speech centres, and a certain stage of organisation having been attained, the opportunity is now afforded for the fuller functional development of the higher centres entrusted with the duty of receiving, discriminating, and co-ordinating the data of the special organs of sense.

The period during which the child is gradually acquiring control over his immediate physical and social environments may roughly be said to extend to the end of his third year.

From that time onwards the worlds of nature and of society for their own sake become objects of curiosity to the child. Every new object presents him with a variety of fresh sensations. He feels, tastes, and bites everything that comes within his reach, and so acquires a world of new experiences. Hence for "the first six years of his life a child has quite enough to do in learning its place in the universe and the nature of its surroundings, and to compel it during any part of that period to give its attention to mere words and symbols is to stint it of the best part of its education for that which is only of secondary importance, and to weaken the foundations of its whole mental fabric."[33]

If, then, during this period the child is left wholly to gather his experiences as he may, he no doubt acquires by his own self-activity a world of new ideas, but the result of this unregulated process will be that the knowledge gained will be largely unsystematised, and much of the experience acquired may be of a nature which may give a false direction to his whole after-development. Hence arise three needs. In the first place, we must endeavour to see that new experiences are presented to the child in some systematic manner, in order that the knowledge may be so organised that it may serve as means to the attainment of ends, and so render future activity more accurate and more efficient. In the second place, we must endeavour to prevent the acquisition of experiences which if allowed to be organised would give an immoral direction to conduct; and in the third place, we must endeavour to establish early in the mind of the child organised systems of means which may hereafter result in the prevalence of activities socially useful to the community.

Now, these three aims are or should be the aims of the Kindergarten School, and we shall now inquire into the ends which the Kindergarten School sets before it, and for this purpose we shall state the fundamental principles which Froebel himself laid down as the guiding principles of this stage of education.

On its intellectual side the Kindergarten as conceived by Froebel has four distinct aims in view. The first aim is by means of comparing and contrasting a series of objects presented in some regular and systematic manner to lead the child to note the likenesses and differences between the things, and so through and by means of his own self-activity to build up coherent and connected systems of ideas. By this method the teacher builds up in the mind of the young child systems of ideas regarding the colours, forms, and other sense qualities of the more common objects of his environment. The second aim is by means of some form of concrete construction to give expression to the knowledge so gained, to make this knowledge more accurate and definite, and thus by a dialectical return to make the experiences of the child definite and accurate, so as to render future action more efficient, and thus pave the way for further progress. The third aim is to utilise the play-activity of the child in the acquisition of new experiences and in their outward concrete expression. The fourth is to engage the child in the production of something socially useful, something which engages his genuine work-activity. In short, what Froebel clearly realised was that the mere taking in of new experiences by the child mind in any order was not sufficient. Experiences to be useful for efficient action must be assimilated—must be organised into a system—and in order that this may be possible the experiences must be presented in such a manner as will render them capable of being organised. Moreover, this mere taking in of new experiences is not enough. There must be a giving out or expression of the knowledge acquired, for it is only in so far as we can turn to use new experiences that we can be sure that they are really ours. Now, since the forms of expression natural to the young child are those which evoke his practical constructive efforts, all outward expression in its earlier stages must assume a concrete form. The aim of the so-called "Gifts" in Froebel's scheme is to build up an organised system of sense-knowledge; the aim of the "Occupations" of the Kindergarten is to develop the power of concrete expression of the child. The "Gifts" and the "Occupations" are correlative methods,—the one concerned with the taking in, the other with the outward expression of the same experience,—and throughout either aspect of the process the reason-activity of the child must be evoked both in the acquisition and in the expression of the new experience. Physiologically, this twofold process implies that during the Kindergarten period the sensory areas of the brain are being exercised and organised and that the associative activity evoked is concerned with the co-ordination of the impressions derived through these areas. Psychologically, it implies that during this period we are mainly concerned with the formation of perceptual systems of knowledge composed of data derived through the special senses and through the active movements of the hands and limbs. Such a process, moreover, is a necessary preliminary for the full after-development of the higher association centres of the brain and for the formation by the mind of conceptual systems of knowledge.

For if we attempt prematurely to exercise the higher centres before the lower have reached a certain measure of development, if we attempt to form conceptual systems of knowledge, such as all language and number systems are, without first laying a sound perceptual basis, then we may do much to hinder future mental growth, if we do not even inflict a positive injury to the child. For the education of the senses neglected, "all after-education partakes of a drowsiness, a haziness, and an insufficiency which it is impossible to cure."[34]

On its moral and social side the aims of the Kindergarten School are no less important. If left to follow the naive instinctive needs of his nature and to gather experiences where and how he may, the child is likely to make acquisitions which later may issue in wrong conduct. Hence one aim of the Kindergarten is to present experiences which may eventually issue in right conduct, and to prevent the acquisition of experiences of an immoral kind. Hence also its insistence upon the need of carefully selecting the environment of the young child, so that as far as possible its early experiences—its first acquisitions—shall be of a healthy nature. Moreover, by means of the organised activities of the school, and by utilising the play-instinct of the child, it seeks to form and establish certain habits of future social worth to the community and to the individual. For, by means of the games and occupations of the Kindergarten School, the child may first of all learn what it means to co-operate with his fellows for a common end or purpose; may learn to submit to authority which he dimly and imperfectly, it may be, perceives to be reasonable; may be trained to habits of accuracy, of order, and of obedience. Above all, the Kindergarten system may rouse and foster in the mind of the child that sense of a corporate life and of a common social spirit the prevalence of which in after-life is the only secure foundation of society.

In England the extreme importance of the education of the infant mind has been, in recent years, clearly acknowledged. The new regulations of the Board of Education no longer allow children under five years of age to be included as "an integral part of a three-R grant-earning Elementary School." A special curriculum has been set forth for their education. They are to have opportunities provided "for the free development of their bodies and minds and for the formation of habits of obedience and attention."[35] What are known as "Kindergarten Occupations are not merely pleasant pastimes for children: if so regarded, they are not intelligently used by the teacher. Their purpose is to stimulate intelligent individual effort, to furnish training of the senses of sight and touch, to promote accurate co-ordination of hand movements with sense impressions, and, not least important, to implant a habit of obedience."

"Formal teaching, even by means of Kindergarten Occupations, is undesirable for children under five. At this stage it is sufficient to give the child opportunity to use his senses freely. To attempt formal teaching will almost inevitably mean, with some of the children, either restraint or over-stimulation, with constant danger to mental growth and health."[36]

From these extracts from the *Suggestions for the Consideration of Teachers* of the Head of the English Board of Education, it will be evident that the spirit of the "Kindergarten" now largely enters into the curriculum of the infant classes. In the future we may hope to see it carried further and that no formal teaching of the child will be undertaken during the first six years of his life. Further, we may hope to see in the future the infant departments of our schools more thoroughly organised than they are at present on the Kindergarten principle, and the curriculum of the Infant School so devised that it shall fit into and pave the way for the curriculum of the Elementary School. For at the earlier stage much may be done by the methods of the Kindergarten to lay the basis for the teaching of the arts of reading, writing, and arithmetic which it is the main business of the Primary School to lead the child to acquire. *E.g.*, at the earlier stage, by the breaking up and reconstructing of concrete groups of things, the child can be initiated into the meaning of a number system. By means of pictures and of concrete forms he can be made gradually acquainted with alphabetic forms, and this teaching lays the basis for the future acquisition of the abstract symbols of printed and written words.

But while much has been done in England to recognise the importance of the early education of the child for the after moral and social good both of the individual and of the community, and to place the instruction of the infant classes in the Public Elementary Schools upon a rational basis, little attention has been paid in Scotland to this subject. As a rule, children in that country do not enter school before the age of five, and there is no separate provision made for the teaching of children under that age; in fact, all scholars under seven years of age are classified together and form the Junior Division of the school.

Such a state of matters reflects but little credit on the educational leaders of Scotland, and indicates an imperfect conception of the real nature of the educative process. For if education is the process of acquiring and organising experiences in order to render future action more efficient, it is surely the height of folly to allow the young child to gather his early experiences as he may. Moreover, in the case of the children of the slums, to allow them during their early years to gather into their brain without any correcting agency "all the sights and scenes of a slum is sheer social madness." "The child must be removed, or partially removed, from such an atmosphere, since it has reached the imitative stage, and is nearing the selective stage of life. For the moment he imitates anything; presently he will imitate what pleases him, what gives him momentary pleasure. Before the unmoral selective stage is reached, the stage which inevitably precedes the moral and immoral selective stage, it is essential that children should receive definite and deliberate guidance, that the imitative faculty should be controlled."[37] In the case of the children of the poorer districts this can be done only through the agency of the Infant School. Much may be done by making the instruction of the school attractive, to counteract the evil influences of the home and social environment, and to lead the child to acquire and organise experiences which will issue in moral and not in immoral conduct.

Hence what we need in the poorer districts of our large towns is Free Kindergarten Schools from which all formal teaching of the three R's is abolished, where for several hours in each day the child may be trained to use his senses in the accurate discrimination and accurate systematisation of sense knowledge; where he may have his constructive activities evoked by the expression in concrete form of what he has been led to perceive through the medium of the senses; where he may be trained to habits of order, of cleanliness, of submission to authority; and where for a time, at least, he may be accustomed to live in a purer and healthier atmosphere than he can find at home or in the street, and where for a brief space he may have that feeling of home which he cannot find at home.[38]

The establishment in the poorer districts of our great towns of schools whose education follows the method of the Kindergarten if accompanied by some system of feeding the child would do much to secure the after social efficiency of the rising generation, and would by its reaction on the home-life tend gradually to raise the ideals of the very poor.

FOOTNOTES:

[33] *The Nervous System and Education,* by Sir James Crichton Browne, *ibid.* p. 345.

[34] *The Nervous System and Education,* by Sir James Crichton Browne, *ibid.* p. 345.

[35] Cf. on this subject the chapter on "School Nurseries" in *National Education and National Life,* ibid.

[36] *Suggestions for the Consideration of Teachers,* chap. iii. (issued by the English Board of Education).

[37] Montmorency's *National Education and National Life,* ibid. p. 143. The chapter on "School Nurseries" should be read by everyone, and especially by every Scotsman interested in the education of young children.

[38] Cf. Charles Lamb's Essay on *Popular Fallacies.*

CHAPTER XI

THE AIM OF THE PRIMARY SCHOOL

During the past thirty years no part of our educational system has received so much attention as the Elementary Schools of the country. If we compare the condition of things which prevails at the present time with that which existed previous to 1870, there can be no doubt that a great advance has been made both in the better provision of the means of education and in the efficiency of the instruction given. Previous to 1870 a large number of the children of the poor received no education.[39] Of those attending school many left with but a scanty knowledge. Now practically every child[40] receives a training in the primary arts of reading, writing, and arithmetic; and with the gradual extension of the period during which the child must attend school, it has become possible to ensure that a larger and larger number of children leaving our Elementary Schools have received an education which may be of value for the after-fulfilment of the simpler practical ends of life. Again, previous to 1870 the school buildings were in many cases unfit for their purpose; now the Elementary Schools of the country both in their building arrangements and equipment are as a rule much superior to the voluntary and endowed schools providing secondary education. Previous to 1870 anyone was thought good enough to undertake the work of teaching; since that time more and more attention has been paid to the qualifications of the teacher and to securing that he shall have attained a certain standard of education, and have received a certain measure of training before engaging upon the work of the instruction of the young. We, *e.g.*, no longer entrust the instruction of the younger children in the school to the older, as was the custom under the monitorial system of Bell and Lancaster, and with the abolition of the pupil-teacher the last remnant of a system introduced at the beginning of the nineteenth century, as the only remedy to meet the dire educational necessities of the time, will have been removed.

But in spite of the great advances which have been made, there is a deep-seated feeling now beginning to find expression, that somehow or other the

Elementary School has not realised all the expectations that were once thought likely to result from the universal education of the children of the nation, and that in particular the Primary School has failed to foster and to establish the moral and social qualities necessary for the welfare of a State whose government is founded on the representative principle.

This, it seems to me, is largely due to the wrong conception of the aims which the Primary School is intended to realise—a conception which prevailed for many years after the introduction of compulsory elementary education. For some time now, and especially during the past few years, a counter-reaction has set in against the narrowness of the aims of the preceding period, and like all reactions it tends to go to the opposite extreme, and so to broaden the aims of the Primary School as to be in danger of failing to realise efficiently any one of the ends which it sets before it.

The state of things immediately preceding 1870 not unnaturally gave rise to the idea that the acquisition of the arts of reading, writing, and arithmetic was the one indispensable object to be attained in the elementary education of the child. This conviction was strengthened by the system of Government grants introduced into both English and Scotch schools, payments to school managers being largely based upon the successes obtained in passes in the three elementary subjects.

Certain results naturally followed. In the first place, no provision was made for the special education of the infant classes. Since the after-success of the child was measured by his attainments in the three R's, the sooner the infant mind was introduced to these subjects the better the after-result might be expected to be. Thus the grant-earning capacity of the child became the teacher's chief consideration. In the second place, the energies of the teacher were directed to secure a certain mechanical accuracy in the use of the three elementary arts rather than their intelligent apprehension. As a consequence, these subjects came in time to be thought of as subjects worthy of attainment for their own sake and their acquisition as an end in itself. Hence it was forgotten that the acquisition and organisation of these systems of elementary knowledge are only valuable because they are the indispensable means of all intercourse, of all commerce, and of all culture. Hence also their use as instruments for the after-realisation of many purposes in life tended to be neglected, or at least to fall into the background. Individual teachers, no doubt, in many cases realised the partial error in this conception of the aims of the Primary School, but the demands of Government inspectors and of school authorities, with their rule-of-thumb methods of testing the success of the teacher's work by the percentage of passes gained, tended often to make the teacher, in spite of his better judgment, look upon the child mainly as a three-R grant-earning subject and to consider the chief aim of primary education to be the securing of a certain mechanical proficiency in the use of the three elementary arts.

Under such a method of examination it was certainly necessary for the teacher to pay some attention to the individuality of the child. If his efforts were to be at all successful it was incumbent upon him to discover as early as possible the range of the child's previous knowledge in the three grant-earning subjects and to find out in which of the three the power of acquisition of the child was naturally weak or naturally strong. Where the number of children in a class was large, little individual attention could, of course, be paid to the child, and in such cases the acquisition of the subject was aided by the mechanical drilling of sections of the class and by recourse to all manner of devices for ensuring the accurate acquisition of the essential subjects.

As a result of this partial and one-sided conception little attention was paid to the use to which these subjects may be put in the realisation of the practical ends of life. Arithmetic, *e.g.*, seemed to the child to be made up of a number of kinds of arithmetic, each process having its own rules and methods of procedure; but it never entered into his mind, and but seldom into that of his teacher, that the various arithmetical processes are at bottom but diverse forms of the one fundamental process of adding to or subtracting from a group. Proportion was one kind of arithmetic, simple interest another, but that these processes symbolised real group-forming processes, or that they had to do with any of the realities of life, was apprehended, if at all, in the most imperfect and hazy manner.

In a similar manner, the overcoming of the mechanical difficulties of language construction occupied the major portion of the attention of the child during the school period, and the function of language in conveying a knowledge of things and persons and events received but a small share of his attention. Meanings of words were indeed tabulated and learnt by heart, and as a rule the child on examination-day could make a fair show in deluding the inspector that the passage read was intelligently apprehended. In very much the same way, the overcoming of the mechanical difficulties of writing and the drilling of the child to form his letters in a uniform style received the chief share of the school-time devoted to the subject.

The interest and attention of the child having been thus mainly occupied in the overcoming of the mechanical difficulties involved in the learning of the three grant-earning subjects, and little attention having been paid to the use of these arts, it followed that upon the conclusion of the school period the child left the school without any real interests having been established as the result of the educative process.

Moreover, except in so far as by their teaching we may establish habits of order and of accuracy, the three elementary subjects in themselves possess no moral or social intent; hence unless we can make the child realise their value as instruments for the attainment of ends of social worth they in themselves fail to play any important part in the building up of character.

Let me put this in another way. We have defined education as the process of acquiring and systematising experiences that will render future action more efficient, or alternatively it is the process by which we organise and establish in the mind systems of ideas for the attainment of ends. But if we make the acquisition of these elementary arts ends in themselves, then it follows that the more efficient action we seek to realise is the more efficient manipulation of a number system or a language system. If, however, we realise that these arts are but means to the realisation of other ends, then we shall understand that it is the character of the latter which mainly determines the resulting character of the education given.

Partly to this erroneous conception of the real function of the elementary arts, and partly to another cause which we shall mention later, may be attributed the poor results which our Elementary School system has attained in the establishment of interests of moral and social worth. If, moreover, we realise how large a proportion of the children left and still do leave school at an early age, before such interests can be permanently established, and in some cases with anything but an adequate knowledge of the elementary arts necessary for all further progress, we may rather be astonished that so much has been done than so little.

But in the reaction against the narrowness and formalism of our early aims in elementary education, there is a tendency—a strong tendency—at the present time to go to the opposite extreme, and to make the elementary instrumental arts the vehicles for the fostering of real interests at too early a stage. This manifests itself on the one hand in the desire to make all instruction interesting to the child, and on the other to introduce the child prematurely to a knowledge of the real conditions of life, before he can have any intelligent understanding of these conditions. From the barrenness and formalism of the earlier period, we now have the demand made that the school should throughout take into account the real and practical necessities of life.

The former tendency—the tendency to make everything interesting to the child by lessening or minimising the mechanical difficulties and by endeavouring in every way to incite the child to become interested in the content of the lesson—is best exemplified by the character of the school books which we now place in the hands of our children. The latter tendency—the tendency to the premature use of the elementary arts—is exemplified by the craving to make our teaching of arithmetic practical and real from the very beginning.

In the former case, instead of endeavouring to make the process of language construction interesting in itself, we divert the child's attention from the acquiring and organising of the system of language forms to the premature acquirement of the content of language. What results is obvious: the main interest being in the content, the interest in the mechanical construction of the form suffers, and as a consequence the child never attains a full mastery over the instrumental art.

In the latter case we attempt to do two things at the same time in our teaching of arithmetic. In every concrete application of arithmetic there are two interests involved: in the first place, there is the number interest—the interest in the analysing and recombining of a group, undertaken for the sake of the reconstruction itself; in the second place, there is the business or real interest, which the number interest indeed subserves, but the two interests are in no case identical. If we attempt to teach the two together, we as a rule teach both badly. The pupil will have but a hazy idea of the business relation, and will run the risk of imperfectly organising the pure number system. Hence all kinds of impossible problems may be given to the child without raising any suspicion of error in his mind, and such cases furnish certain evidence that the business relation does not really concern him, but that his whole attention is engaged with the purely constructive aspect of number. Another example of the same error of confounding two separate things is the "blind mixture we make of arithmetic and measuring." Because arithmetic is involved in all measuring we assume that when the child can add together feet and inches, therefore he has a complete knowledge of these spatial magnitudes. But manifestly, if spatial magnitude is to be taught intelligently, it must at first be taught independently of the number relation, which is a general system instrumental in the realisation of many concrete interests.

From these considerations, certain general results follow. On the one hand, the earlier conception of the aim of the Primary School as being mainly concerned with the acquirement and organisation of the three elementary arts as ends in themselves must be condemned. Language and number systems are means to the realisation of certain concrete ends of after-life, and the school during the later stages of education must endeavour to lead the child to perceive how these systems may be utilised in the furtherance of these real concrete interests. On the other hand, the attempt to combine prematurely these two aims will result in the imperfect attainment of both. During the earlier stages of education the main interest must be in the construction for its own sake of the language system or the number system, and while the real interest may be introduced it must always be kept subsidiary to the main interest—must first of all be taught for its own sake, and the instrumental art only used for its furtherance in so far as the acquirement of the former is not obstructed. *E.g.*, the placing of geography and history Readers in the hands of the child while he is still struggling with the difficulties of language construction can only result in the history and geography being imperfectly understood and the organisation of the language system being delayed and hindered.

Once the elementary and subsidiary systems have been fairly well organised and established, their function as means for the furtherance of real interests should occupy a larger share of the child's attention and of the time of the school. These real interests, however, must in every case and at every stage be taught at first for their own sake, and thereafter their relation to the instrumental art explained and applied. Gradually, as they become better organised and more firmly established, the elementary arts occupy a smaller and smaller share of attention, until finally they function automatically, and the whole attention can be directed to the furtherance of the real interests to which the elementary arts are the indispensable means.

Hence we note three stages in the elementary education of the child—the stage preceding the formal instruction in the elementary arts; the stage in which the formal instruction should predominate and receive the greater share of the child's attention; the stage in which the elementary systems having been in great measure organised and established, they may be utilised as means to the furtherance of the real interests. The first stage corresponds to the Infant or Kindergarten age: here the main object is to build up in the mind of the child systems of ideas about the things of his environment; to extend, by conversation and by reading to the child, the vocabulary of his own language; to give him practice in the combining and recombining of concrete groups of things, and to introduce him to a knowledge of the various language forms in a concrete shape.

In the second stage, and here the work of the Primary School begins, the main emphasis at the beginning must be laid on the acquirement and establishment of the language and number systems for their own sake. If right methods are followed, the child can be interested in these processes of construction without the need of calling into use at every point some real interest. In the concluding stage the use of these instruments as means to the realisation of the simpler practical ends of life should receive more attention.

One reason, then, for the poor moral and social results effected in the past by our Elementary School system has been the undue emphasis placed upon the acquisition of the merely formal arts to the neglect of the real interests to which the former are but the means. Another cause, however, has been operative in producing this negative result. In the Elementary Schools, in the past, little attention has been paid to the individuality of the child, and little heed given to the differences between children as regards their different rates of intellectual growth and their differing aptitudes for various branches of study. Under a system of classification which compelled each individual, whether intellectually well or moderately or poorly equipped, to advance at an equal rate, attention to the individual with any other aim than to raise the weak to the standard of the average child in acquiring the three R's was impossible. Again, our huge city schools, partly on account of their vast size, partly on the ground that they are unable to organise school games, partly on account of their lack of any common school interests, do not and cannot foster any sense of a corporate life, any feeling of a common social spirit. Where our English Public School system is strong, our Elementary and sometimes even our Day Secondary School systems are weak. If the home fails to foster these qualities, and the school does not or cannot fill the gap, then as a rule we turn out our boys and girls poorly equipped to fulfil their duties in after-life as members of a corporate community and as citizens of a State. Mere teaching of history or of civics in our schools will do little to attain this end, unless by some method or other we can foster by means of the school-life the real civic spirit. It is, of course, easy to point out the nature of the disease; it is more difficult to prescribe a remedy. But much might be done to strengthen and increase the moral influence of the school by a better system of classification, which took into account the differences in intellectual capacity and in natural aptitude, and which as a consequence, in the education of the child, paid more attention to each child's individuality. This would involve much smaller classes than exist at present, and would further involve that the children should be under the care of one teacher for a longer time than is now the rule. At the present time, in many cases, the teacher is employed in teaching the same subjects, at the same stage, year after year, to a yearly fresh batch of sixty or seventy children. Consequently he learns to look upon his pupils as mere subjects to whom must be imparted the required measure of instruction. Of the children in themselves, of their home-life, of their interests outside school, he knows nothing, and as a rule cares less.

If in addition to this we ceased erecting barracks for the instruction of children and erected schools for their education, we should make even a further advance in this direction. If it is impossible for other reasons to lessen the size of our city Elementary Schools, then the remedy lies in the division of the schools into departments in which the Head should be entrusted with the supervision of the education of the children during several years. In this way it would be possible for the teacher to get to know each child individually, to direct his education in accordance with his aptitudes, and to exert an influence over him. Thus, by giving more attention to the organised games of the school and by the creation of school interests, much might be done to remedy the defects of the school on the side of moral and social education. At best, however, when the home fails, the Elementary School can do little, and we must put our trust in the ethical agencies of society to assist and promote the efforts of the school in the furthering of a right social spirit and in the creation of a common corporate feeling.

FOOTNOTES:

[39] *E.g.*, in 1861 it was calculated that only 6 per cent. of the children of the poor in England were receiving a satisfactory elementary education. Cf. Balfour Graham's *Educational System of Great Britain and Ireland*, p. 14.

[40] *E.g.*, in 1872 in Scotland school places were provided for only 8.3 per cent. of the population. In 1905 places were provided for 21.22 of the population. Cf. *Report on Scotch Education*, 1905, p. 6.

CHAPTER XII

THE AIM OF THE SECONDARY SCHOOL

We have seen that on its intellectual side the Primary School has two main functions to perform in the education of the child. In the first place, the school must endeavour to secure that the elementary arts of reading, writing, and arithmetic are well organised and well established in the mind of the child. The more effectively the language and number systems are organised and established the more efficiently will they function in the performance of future action. Moreover, it is only when they have become so organised as to function automatically that they reach their highest efficiency as instruments for the further extension of knowledge or of practice.

In the second place, the Primary School must train the pupil to the use of these systems as instruments for the realisation of other and concrete ends or interests. *E.g.*, the number system may be used in the furtherance of the measuring interest, the weighing interest, and so on. The two dangers we have to avoid are on the one hand the barren formalism of treating the acquisition of these arts as ends in themselves, and on the other of supposing that the real interests can be intelligently understood merely through the instrumentality of the elementary arts and that they do not require independent treatment of themselves.

If the child is destined to go no farther than the Elementary School stage, then at least the concluding year of the school should be mainly devoted to training him to the use of the primary instrumental arts in the establishment of systems of knowledge necessary for the realisation of the simpler practical ends of life.

If, however, the child is selected for a course of higher education, the educative process becomes different in nature. In the first-named case we are content to give the child practice in the application of an already established system to concrete problems. In the second case we endeavour, using the elementary systems as means, to establish other systems of knowledge as means to the attainment of still further ends. We may, *e.g.*, on the basis of the vernacular language build up a foreign language system as a means either to commercial intercourse or to literary culture. In short, the aim of the Secondary School is, using the elementary systems as the basal means, to organise and establish other systems of means for the attainment of the more complex interests of after-life, practical and theoretical. The object of establishing a system of knowledge is not to pass examinations,—this is the schoolmaster's error,—but to render future action more efficient, to further in after-life some complex interest of a practical or theoretical nature. To the few, indeed, the establishment and systematisation of knowledge may be an end in itself. To the many, the systematisation and establishment is and ought to be undertaken as a means to the more efficient furtherance of some practical end. Further, the only justification for the seeking of knowledge for its own sake is that thereby it may be better understood, better established and better systematised, and so become better fitted to make practice more efficient.

Hence the question as regards secondary education resolves itself into the question as to the nature of the systems of knowledge which we should endeavour to establish systematically in the mind of the child, and before we can answer this question we must know the length of time which the child can afford to spend at the Higher School and his possible vocation in after-life. For if education is the process by which the child is led to acquire and organise experiences so as to render future action more efficient, we must know something of the nature of this action, something of the nature of the future social services for which his education is to train him, and the school period must be of sufficient length to enable the required systems to be established permanently and thoroughly.

Neglect of these two obvious considerations has led in the past and even in the present leads to two errors in our organisation of the means of secondary education. In the first place, until quite recently, we have been too much inclined to the opinion that secondary education was all of one type, and even where this error has been recognised, as in Germany, the tendency still exists to emphasise unduly the particular type of education which has as its main ingredients the ancient classical languages. We spend years in the attempt to reconstruct and establish in the mind of the youth a knowledge of these language systems, and in a large number of cases we fail to attain adequately even this end. We build up laboriously systems of means which in after-life function *directly* in the attainment of no end, and as a consequence, in many cases, the dissolution of the system is as rapid as its acquisition was slow. At the time of the Renascence and when first introduced into the curriculum of the Secondary School, these languages, and especially Latin, did then possess a high functional value, since they were the indispensable means to the furtherance of knowledge and to social intercourse. To-day they possess little functional value, and their claim for admission into the school curriculum is chiefly based upon their so-called training and disciplinary values.

Let us consider this for a moment: in the reconstruction of, say, the Latin language, the pupil is being trained in the reconstruction and re-establishment of a language system whose methods and rules of construction are much more complex and intricate than those of any living language, and whose forms are so designed as to bring out exactly varied shades of meaning. Hence, in its acquisition the pupil receives practice in the exact discrimination of the meaning of words, and in their accurate placing and reconstruction within the sentence—the unit of expression—in order to bring out the exact interpretation of the thought or statement of fact intended by the writer.

Further, we may train the pupil during the school period to self-apply the language system in the further interpretation of relatively unknown passages. In short, we can train him in the processes of language construction and of language application. Moreover, in considering this question, we must take into account that during the school period the main interest must necessarily be directed to the acquisition and establishment of the system itself, that little attention can be directed towards the content for its own sake, and that the establishment of the system so that it shall function automatically in the interpretation of the content is a stage which is attained in comparatively few cases, and then only after many years of study.

If we then take into account, and we must take into account, the fact that the chief value of the ancient languages as Secondary School subjects lies in their use as training and disciplinary instruments—that in after-life they function directly in the attainment of no practical end, and only indirectly in so far as the habits acquired of the exact weighing of the meaning of words and of the accurate placing of words are carried over for the attainment of practical ends in which these qualities of exact interpretation and exact expression of language are the chief requisites—we shall understand that while they may be of value in securing the efficient after-performance of certain social services, they play but a small part in the furthering of any service which requires an exact knowledge of the qualities of things and an accurate knowledge of the laws governing the operations of nature.

In the second place, neglect of the fact that the aim of education is to establish systems of means for the efficient after-performance of actions has led us to neglect the fact that in the acquisition and establishment of systems of knowledge we require to limit the scope of our aims and to carry on the process of education during a period sufficiently extended to admit of the stable establishment of the systems. If, *e.g.*, we attempt to establish too many systems, then as a result we often stably establish none, with the further result that after the school period has passed the knowledge gained soon disappears. If, again, we attempt in too limited a time to establish an elaborate and complex system of knowledge, as *e.g.* that of the Latin language, then we never reach the stage when it can be self-applied intelligently in the furtherance of any end. Hence, if a boy leaves the Elementary School and enters upon a High School course with the intention of leaving at the age of fifteen or sixteen and entering upon some employment, the systems of knowledge which can be established during the school period must be different from those of the boy whose education is intended to be extended until twenty-one. If, then, a national system of education is to make adequate provision for the efficient after-performance of the various social services which the nation requires at the hands of its adult members; if, in short, it is to be organic to the life of the State as a whole, then there must be not one type of higher education but several; for it is to her Higher Schools that a nation must principally look for the preparation of citizens who in after-life will discharge the more important services of the community. This truth has already been realised in other countries, notably Germany. We are only beginning to realise it, and to take measures to carry it into practice.

Moreover, in a national system of education we shall need not one system of advancing means but several; not merely an educational ladder that may carry the boy to the University, but also educational steps by which the individual may mount to the Technical or the Commercial or the Art College.

Hence our aims in the higher education of the youth, and as a consequence the nature of the systems of knowledge which we should endeavour to organise and to establish in their minds, will vary in accordance with the nature of the service which in adult life the boy is likely to perform. Now, these services may be divided into four main classes.

In the first place, every nation requires an army of efficient industrial workers. Partly, in some cases, owing to the decline of the apprenticeship system, partly owing to the fact that where apprentices are still employed no systematic measures are taken to instruct the youth in the principles underlying his particular art, it is becoming increasingly necessary that the school should supply and supplement the knowledge required for the efficient after-performance of the industrial and technical arts. Hence one kind of Higher School urgently required is the Trade or Technical School. In a large number of cases this need could be supplied by Evening Continuation Schools. At present, however, our Evening Schools are too predominantly commercial and literary, and do not make adequate provision for the trade and technical needs of the community. Further, we must endeavour to secure that the boy or girl enters the Evening Continuation School as soon after he leaves the Elementary School as possible. For in many cases at the present time the boy after leaving the Primary School loafs at night about the streets, and in a short time through disuse forgets much of what he learned at school, and often in addition acquires habits which tend to unfit him for any future strenuous effort. When, therefore, he feels the need for more knowledge in order to advance in his trade, the Evening School has too frequently to begin by doing over again the work of the Elementary School before it can enter upon the work of establishing the higher system of knowledge.

In the second place, a nation such as ours requires a trained body of servants for the efficient carrying on of her commerce. Preparation for the simpler forms of service could be furnished by the commercial classes of the Evening Continuation Schools. For preparation for the higher services, we require a type of school which beginning after the Elementary School stage has been completed, carries on the boy's education until the fifteenth or sixteenth year, whose chief aim should be to lay a sound basis in the acquisition and organisation of one or two modern languages and in the acquirement of the arts instrumental for the carrying on of commercial transactions. Further means of advance in these studies should be provided by the day or evening Commercial College.

In the third place, every modern nation requires a trained body of scientific workers for the after carrying on of her industrial and technical arts. Hence we need a type of school which by making the physical sciences their chief object of study prepare the way for the future training of the student in the application of scientific knowledge to the furtherance of the industrial and technical arts.

Lastly, we require a type of secondary education which shall prepare the boy for the efficient discharge of the duties which the State requires at the hands of her physicians, her theologians, her jurists.

Thus, since all education is the acquisition of experiences that will render future action more efficient, the nature of the secondary education given must depend on the nature of the services to which the systems of knowledge are the means. A classical education may be a good preparation for the after-discharge of the duties of the theologian or the jurist; it certainly will not do much for the efficient discharge of the duties of the mechanical engineer and the practical chemist.

But one error must be avoided. Whilst the various types of Secondary School must fashion their curricula according to the nature of the services for which they prepare, we must not forget that the school has other duties to perform than the mere preparation for the social services by which a man hereafter earns his living. It must in every case endeavour to organise and establish those systems of means necessary for the after-discharge of the civic duties of life and instrumental for the right use of leisure.

Practically we need three types of Higher School—one in which modern languages form the basal subjects of the curriculum; one in which the physical sciences are the main systems organised and established; one in which the classical languages form the main staple of education.

CHAPTER XIII

THE AIM OF THE UNIVERSITY

"All public institutions of learning are called into existence by social needs, and first of all by technical practical necessities. Theoretical interests may lead to the founding of private associations such as the Greek philosophers' schools; public schools owe their origin to the social need for professional training. Thus during the Middle Ages the first schools were called into being by the need of professional training for ecclesiastics, the first learned profession, and a calling whose importance seemed to demand such training. Essentially the same necessity called into being the Universities of the Parisian type, with their artistic and theological faculties. The two other types of professional schools, the law school and the medical school, which were first developed in Italy, then united with the former. The Universities therefore originated as a union of 'technical' schools for ecclesiastics, jurists, and physicians, to which division the faculty of Arts was related as a general preparatory school, until during the nineteenth century it also assumed something of the character of a professional institution for the training of teachers for the Secondary School."[41]

Thus the early aim of the University was, as it still continues to be, to provide the training for the after-supply of those services which the State requires at the hands of her theologians, her jurists, and her physicians. In Germany, and to some extent even in our own country, the Arts faculty of the University is ceasing to perform the function of a General Preparatory School to the professional schools, and is becoming an independent school, having for its aim the preparation of teachers for the Intermediate and Secondary Schools of the country. In Scotland, indeed, it serves at the present time as a Preparatory School mainly to the theological faculty. As the Secondary Schools of the country become more efficient, better differentiated, and better organised, the need of a Preparatory School within our Universities will gradually become less, and the University will be able to devote more of her energies to the training of students preparing for some one or other of the above-named professions. With this change the philosophical studies of the Arts faculty will become increasingly important, and the method of teaching the linguistic and scientific studies receive a larger share of attention than they do at present.

But the other and perhaps the more important function of the University is to carry on and to extend the work of scientific and literary research for its own sake. This is the dominant note of the German and American Universities of to-day. The emphasis is laid not so much upon their function as schools for the supply of certain professional services, but upon them as great national laboratories for the extension of knowledge and the betterment of practice. In Great Britain, and especially in Scotland, this conception of the function of the University has not received the same prominence as, *e.g.*, in Germany, where the intimate union of scientific investigation and professional instruction gives the German Universities their peculiar character. Indeed, in the latter country the tendency at the present time is rather to over-emphasise the function of the Universities in furthering scientific and literary research to the neglect of the other and no less important aim. Two dangers must be avoided. In the first place, whenever the chief emphasis is laid upon the Universities as mainly schools for professional training, the teaching tends to become narrow and dogmatic. The teacher ceasing to be an investigator, gradually loses touch with the spirit of the age, and as a consequence he fails adequately to perform the duty of efficiently training his students for their after life-work. In the second place, when the emphasis is laid strongly upon the function of the University as an institution for the carrying on of scientific and literary research there is the danger of again lapsing into the old fallacy that knowledge for knowledge' sake is an end in itself, that the object of education is to acquire and organise systems of means which function in the attainment of no practical end, and that the acquisition of knowledge is valuable for the culture of the individual mind apart from any social purpose which the knowledge subserves.

The University must therefore ever keep in view the two aims, of advancing knowledge not for its own sake but in order that future action may be rendered more efficient, and of adequately training for professional services.

But to the older professions for which the University prepares there have been added during the past century other vocations or professions which need and demand an education no less important and no less thorough than the education for the well established recognised professions. The need for the higher training of the future leaders of industry and the future captains of commerce has been provided by the organisation and establishment of technological schools and colleges. The establishment and organisation of the "Technical University" has been more thorough in Germany than in this country. There we find established newer institutions, of which the Charlottenburg College is the best known and most important, for the higher education of those intended in after-life to perform the more important industrial services of the community. These institutions both in their organisation and instruction are constantly approximating in type to the older Universities.

The recently established Universities in the North of England attempt, with what success it is too early yet to declare, to combine both aims of training for the older and newer professions. In Scotland the latter work is largely undertaken by the Technical Colleges, and in these institutions the increasing need is for the extension and development of the Day-school course.

One other question of some importance remains for brief consideration. In our own country, but more especially in Germany, there is a tendency at the present time to effect a complete separation between the work of the University and the work of the Technical College.

This separation has arisen partly through the operation of external historical conditions, but it has also arisen partly through the tendency in certain academic circles to look down upon technical knowledge and ability as something inferior. The exclusiveness and the torpor of the older Universities in many cases has been a further cause tending to the creation of the Technical College separated from the University.

Such a separation, however, is good neither for the University nor for the Technical College. The former in carrying out the aim of scientific research and of the extension of knowledge requires ever the vivifying touch of actual concrete experience, and this it can only obtain by keeping in close contact with those whose chief function is the application of scientific knowledge to practice. The latter in carrying out its more practical aims requires, if it is to be saved from the narrowness of mere specialisation and from degenerating into empirical methods, the constant co-operation of those whose outlook is not narrowed down to the immediate practical end, but takes in the subject as a whole, and whose chief function is the better systematisation of knowledge.

Hence, while the aim of the University is different from that of the Technical College, they are so intimately correlated that neither can reach its fullest development without the aid and co-operation of the other. The Technical Colleges should be the professional schools attached to the scientific side of the Universities. Moreover, this division and separation is economically wasteful, since the general training in science which must precede the practical training has to be carried on both in the University and in the Technical College.

In Scotland this separation has not advanced to such a stage as is the case in Germany. In any further reorganisation of university and higher education it is earnestly to be hoped that the Day Technical College will find its rightful place as an integral part of the University, and that the latter may realise that her function is to further and extend the bounds of knowledge in order that practice in every sphere of life may be rendered more efficient.

FOOTNOTE:

[41] Cf. Prof. Paulsen, *The German Universities*, p. 111 (Eng. Trans.).

CHAPTER XIV

CONCLUSION—THE PRESENT PROBLEMS IN EDUCATION

The first necessity of the present for teachers and for all concerned with the upbringing of children is to realise the true meaning of education—that it is the process by which we lead the child to acquire and organise experiences that will render future action more efficient; that by our educational agencies we seek to establish systems of knowledge that shall hereafter function in the efficient performance of services of social value; and that the only method which really educates and can educate is the method which evokes the constructive activity of reason in the establishment of the various systems of means. Education does not aim at culture nor at knowledge for its own sake, but at fitting the individual for social service. Our school system tends ever to forget this truth. It is in constant danger of losing sight of this ultimate aim of education by keeping its attention too narrowly fixed on some nearer and proximate aim. It tends often to lay too much stress on mere examinations and examination results. It forgets that the only true test of knowledge gained lies in the pupil's ability to use it intelligently in the furtherance of some purpose—and of some social purpose, and that the ultimate test of a system of education is the kind of social individual it turns out. If our educational system turns out boys and girls who in after-life become efficient workers, efficient citizens, and men and women who have learned how to use their leisure rightly, then it has fulfilled its function. If, on the other hand, it fails in a large number of cases to attain these three ends or any one of them, however it may satisfy the other tests applied, it has not performed its function, is not a system which is "organic" to the welfare of the State.

The second necessity is to realise the true place of the school as the formal agent in the education of the child. Mankind by a long and laborious process has discovered and established many systems of knowledge. He has created language and invented arts for the realisation of the many purposes of life. It is the business of the school to impart this knowledge to the child—to put him in possession at least of some part of this heritage which has come down to him, and to do so in such a manner that while acquiring the experience he shall also be trained in the method of finding and establishing systems of means for himself and by himself. If, however, we lay the emphasis on the mere imparting of the garnered experiences of the ages, the danger to be feared is lest our teaching degenerate into mere dogmatism or mere cram. If, on the other hand, we lay too much emphasis on the ability to self-find and self-establish systems, we are in danger of losing sight of the social purpose of all knowledge—of forgetting that the only justification for establishing a system of knowledge is that it may efficiently function in the attainment of some purpose of life.

Of the more important of the practical problems of our own day and generation the first and most important is to realise that our educational system as it exists at present is not fitted to produce and maintain an efficient and sufficient supply of all the social services which the modern State requires of its adult members, and that we must consider this question of education as a whole and in all its parts, and quite clear of mere party interests. Above all, we must get over the fatal habit of reforming one part of the system and leaving the other parts alone. The whole problem of education from the Primary School to the University requires consideration and organisation. We reform now our Universities, then after a period our Secondary School system, and so we proceed, advancing here, retrograding there, but of education as an organically connected whole we have no thought.

But apart from the want of organisation as a whole our educational system in its parts is at present defective. We require to reconsider the question of how best to educate the children of the very poor. At present we fail in a large number of cases to train up the children of this class to be socially efficient. Economically and morally we fail to reach any high standard. No doubt the home and social environment is all against the school influence; but by a more rational system of early education, by taking more care of the physical development of the child, and, if need be, for a time, making public provision for the feeding of the children of the very poor, we might do much to remove this defect. Above all, we must endeavour to stem the yearly flow of boys and girls at the conclusion of the Primary School period into mere casual and unskilled employments, and must endeavour by some means or other to continue the education of the child for some years further.

Again, we require to make better provision for the technical training of our workmen. By a system of Evening Continuation Schools having as their aim the instruction of the youth in the arts underlying or subsidiary to his particular calling, we might do much to amend this defect. Moreover, the Evening Continuation Schools might play a much more important part than they now do in the securing of the future moral and civic efficiency of the individual and of the nation.

Lastly, and this need is clearly felt by all acquainted with the subject, we require the development and extension of our Technical Colleges, in order that we may adequately train those whose duty in after-life will be the application of advanced scientific knowledge in the furtherance of the arts and industries of life.

www.ingramcontent.com/pod-product-compliance
Lightning Source LLC
Chambersburg PA
CBHW081117080526
44587CB00021B/3628